1007278060

Google This!

CHANDOS
INFORMATION PROFESSIONAL SERIES

Series Editor: Ruth Rikowski
(E-mail: Rikowskigr@aol.com)

Chandos' new series of books is aimed at the busy information professional. They have been specially commissioned to provide the reader with an authoritative view of current thinking. They are designed to provide easy-to-read and (most importantly) practical coverage of topics that are of interest to librarians and other information professionals. If you would like a full listing of current and forthcoming titles, please visit www.chandospublishing.com or email wp@woodheadpublishing.com or telephone +44(0) 1223 499140.

New authors: we are always pleased to receive ideas for new titles; if you would like to write a book for Chandos, please contact Dr Glyn Jones on email gjones@chandospublishing.com or telephone +44 (0) 1993 848726.

Bulk orders: some organisations buy a number of copies of our books. If you are interested in doing this, we would be pleased to discuss a discount. Please contact on email wp@woodheadpublishing.com or telephone +44(0) 1223 499140.

Google This!

Putting Google and other social media sites to work for your library

TERRY BALLARD

CHANDOS
PUBLISHING

Oxford Cambridge New Delhi

Chandos Publishing
Hexagon House
Avenue 4
Station Lane
Witney
Oxford OX28 4BN
UK
Tel: +44 (0) 1993 848726
E-mail: info@chandospublishing.com
www.chandospublishing.com
www.chandospublishingonline.com

Chandos Publishing is an imprint of Woodhead Publishing Limited

Woodhead Publishing Limited
80 High Street
Sawston, Cambridge CB22 3HJ
UK
Tel: +44 (0) 1223 499140
Fax: +44 (0) 1223 832819
www.woodheadpublishing.com

First published in 2012

ISBN: 978-1-84334-677-7 (print)
e-ISBN: 978-1-78063-317-6 (online)

British Library Cataloguing-in-Publication Data.
A catalogue record for this book is available from the British Library.

Typeset by Domex e-Data Pvt. Ltd.
Printed in the UK and USA.

With love to my wife Donna:

From the Googleplex to long nights at home,
she was a part of this project every inch of the way

"Official culture still strives to force the new media to do the work of the old media. But the horseless carriage did not do the work of the horse; it abolished the horse and did what the horse could never do. The audience, as ground, shapes and controls the work of art."

– Marshall McLuhan, educator and philosopher

"A good hockey player plays where the puck is. A great hockey player plays where the puck is going to be."

– Wayne Gretzky, ice hockey professional

"Everything works if you let it."

– Meat Loaf, rock singer

Contents

List of figures

Acknowledgements

This has been an amazing year as I approach my 50th anniversary of working in libraries. Thanks to a contract with Chandos Publishing, I got to talk to people in libraries and information technology that have done the most and shone the brightest. It's hard to know where to begin, but I'll start with Google.

Karen Wickre (now with Twitter) liked the idea and invited me to the Googleplex, Google's headquarters in Mountain View, California. Sean Carlson from the New York office met with me and began a plan for spending my day in Mountain View wisely. Rachel Durfee coordinated that on the California end and guided us through an utterly amazing day. Product managers Anurag Acharya, Michael Bolognino, James Crawford, Rajat Mukherjee and Phil Mui filled my head with new ideas while Donna furiously took notes.

Later that day we had a very useful visit with Jacques Herbert of YouTube, learning how the site is pursuing serious goals in education. The next month I was invited to the New York office again to meet with Sean and his colleagues Jesse Friedman and Susan Cadreche to discuss issues in Google Maps and Google Earth.

My only face-to-face interview outside of California was with Johannes Neuer, eCommunications Manager for the New York Public Library, who was totally proud of how his library had made a massive impact on all areas of social media. It was also an extreme honor to interview people like

Colin Wight, Senior Content Manager at the British Library, as well as Helena Zinkham and Michelle Springer from the Library of Congress. Also Jasmine deGaia, who is a driving force behind social media at OCLC. Harrison Dekker from the University of California Berkeley was helpful in explaining why he developed the largest example of a Google Custom Search that I've seen to date. Marie Radford and Chirag Shah gave a useful academic perspective on social media.

Jeff Dawson of the Lester Public Library in Two Rivers, Wisconsin, Karen Perone and Amanda Dias of the Rodman Public Library, Christina Crocker and Marcia Blackman of the East Meadow Public Library, Brian Herzog, and David Newyear from the Mentor Public Library were all generous with sharing information.

To paraphrase Forrest Gump, getting an editor is like a box of chocolates. I got the best with editor Jonathan Davis and his assistant George Knott. Their patience and enthusiasm for the project will never be forgotten.

Thanks to Marilyn Johnson for her encouragement in this project. Her wildly popular 2010 book *This Book is Overdue! How Librarians and Cybrarians Can Save Us All* was a major inspiration for *Google This!* Instead of repeating what others had written, she went out and talked to librarians of all types.

Also, a special nod to my very distinguished colleague at New York Law School, James Grimmelmann. When I mentioned his name at Google, doors started opening.

Thanks to Alexis Rossi of the Internet Archive for taking the time explaining their mission, and for her hospitality at the San Francisco main office.

Finally, for the people who promised to give me material and didn't, well, you know who you are. In three cases I mentioned your work anyway because it was important. I hope you enjoy the book.

Foreword

Google. It's difficult to think of a time when there was an Internet without it. Google is a phenomenon. What began as a research project by two university students blossomed in to a multi-billion dollar company. And more.

Today, the word *google* itself is synonymous with search, find, look-up. You may not yet *google* your car keys or glasses, but someday that notion may not be so far fetched. For finding information or even asking everyday questions, Google is the only tool most people think of.

Online life before Google was chaotic. In the early 1990s, information on the Internet was exploding at exponential rates. The World Wide Web provided access to information as well a common way for that information to be displayed. But it wasn't perfect.

The problem? There was no index. In one of my books published at the time, I wrote, "The Internet is like a vast library without a card catalog or librarian."

Indeed, back before the Internet, if you wanted to know something you were told to visit a library. There you could find more than books. There were references, movies, music, and often history itself. Imagine my thrill when I discovered Special Collections.

Then there's the knowledge of the library staff. I was blown away when someone told me that you could simply ask a librarian if you wanted to know the answer to any question: I remember phoning up the city library to ask why the game of Ping Pong was called Ping Pong. (The librarian, who happened to be of Chinese decent, immediately knew the answer: the game is named after the sound the ball makes.)

If you visit Google today and type in, "why is it called ping pong," you'll find the same answer. Google was able to give me that answer in 0.21 seconds. So not only is Google the Internet's library card catalog, it's also a pretty spiffy librarian.

The Internet is more than just Google. It's also becoming a social environment. Tools such as Facebook, Twitter, YouTube, Flickr, and more build online communities. There are social networks of people and places, a locus of activities. At the speed of the Internet, and coupled with ubiquitous mobile devices, information is being shared faster and more broadly than at any other time in human history.

That can be intimidating.

Change is a continuing part of the Internet and the new, mobile-connected society. It's important that those of us who provide information stay in tune and on top of things as they happen. So people often ask me, "How can you keep up with all this changing information?"

The curious thing is that to meet that end, I use the very tools that are evolving and appearing every day. That may sound scary, but once you're in the loop, and learn where to go to find current information and resources, it's actually easy. In fact, it's addictive. And it's necessary if you want to exist and prosper in a culture where another Google looms in the wings, ready to take over and change the world.

Armed with the tools described in this book, you can augment your skills and help bring your library into the twenty-first century. After all, the social hub of Internet activities belongs in the heart of your community, which is the local library. It's the next logical step in the information revolution.

Dan Gookin, 2012
Author of the first *For Dummies* title, *DOS For Dummies*, and many other technology titles

Preface

"We learn from history that we've learned nothing from history."

– George Bernard Shaw, playwright

Fast Forward

Mountain View, California is a mid-sized town near San Jose that is just oozing with good Karma. In four blocks of Castro Street you will find independent book stores, an Asian store to take care of all of your Buddha needs, about 20 restaurants serving some form of oriental food, a few Mexican restaurants, and a shop that sells specialty beads. On a warm late September day we took our time to choose a restaurant. It was hard to think of food. Tomorrow we would be going to the Googleplex, Google's headquarters.

I had tried filling out a form that went to Google's press office, describing this book. There was no response. One of my colleagues at New York Law School is James Grimmelmann, one of the world's leading authorities on the Google Book Settlement. I asked him if he could give me a contact name at Google. Minutes later, somebody from Google wrote back to me, and forwarded my message to Karen Wickre in their press relations department. She asked me if I had any plans to travel to California to visit Google.

I had not, but it didn't take long to make plans. My wife said that this is the librarians' equivalent of finding the Golden Wonka Ticket.

I had already spent a day with Sean Carlson in the company's massive New York office. Sean had very carefully listened to my plans for the book and made a list of the type of people I should be meeting. He assured me that I would have plenty to do in my day at the Googleplex. The week before the visit, I was exchanging emails with Rachel Durfee in Communications. She wrote out a plan for a general tour, followed by five interviews with product managers.

On 20 September 2011, we drove into the Googleplex parking lot (plenty of spaces – Googlers are usually not morning people). Rachel met us at the door and got us our name tags. Then we crossed the street from the Communications building to the main campus. There is no one giant building there, but a number of four-story structures. Smiling, energetic young people are dashing from place to place. Many of them have smiling, energetic dogs in tow (Golden Retrievers are the canine of choice). What followed was likely the most intense five hours of my life.

In hour-long sessions, I talked to product managers in relation to Google Books, Custom Search, Scholar, Blogger, and Analytics. Each one of these sessions resulted in exciting revelations that ended up in the pages of this book. There was intense synergy as Google Power User interacted with Google Product Manager. The word "wow" was heard frequently. My wife Donna came along to take notes for me, so I wouldn't have to look up and down. This turned out to be a fabulous idea. After our last interview at the Googleplex, we drove south to San Bruno to meet the educational projects manager of YouTube.

That day was the culmination of a long quest to use technology to bring information to the people who needed it.

A witness to the revolution

You may think it odd to even mention the pre-automation past in a book about the furiously changing world of online tools, but I have my reasons. Students who graduate in the 2012 class of library school have lived their entire lives with computers constantly enhancing their information needs. Unless they studied it in a library history class, they probably couldn't imagine a library where the most important information tool was a 3 × 5 inch card. You can't know where you are going if you don't know where you have been.

My first day working in a library was in early September of 1966. I was hired by the Phoenix Public Library as a part-time clerk, and then as a paraprofessional. At that time, the most advanced technology in the building was the photocopy machine. By the 1980s, libraries were starting to think about moving away from card catalogs and towards an electronic solution. The library signed on with OCLC (Online Computer Library Center) in Dublin, Ohio, who used its giant computers to keep track of our library's holdings. In 1988, I developed an interest in the use of personal computers for library work, and I went to the University of Arizona to get my master's degree in library science. I then moved to New York to begin work as a university systems librarian – just in time for things to change dramatically.

What is inside

The Internet was coming into view in the late 1980s just as I was finishing my library degree and lining up a systems librarian position on Long Island; however, many of us look back to the early 1960s when Theodor Holm Nelson invented the term *hypertext*, to describe how data can be stored in a way that is not hierarchical, but more attuned to the way people think. He envisioned an operation called *Xanadu*, which would store all of the world's information and make it available through hypertext. (Does this sound familiar?) At the time, however, there were no computers that could fulfill his vision, so he went on to be an independent thinker who was so disappointed with the World Wide Web that he did not want to claim paternity. In the early to mid 1990s we were slow to realize that we were in the beginning of the ultimate information revolution. By 2010, I had found that using a Google Custom Search that only indexed respected legal sources could be a popular addition to our web pages, in addition to attracting a large following outside the campus. I will tell the story of how we developed these specialized engines and, more importantly, give step-by-step directions for creating your own engine. Neither of the libraries I've worked for since 1997 has made a major commitment to Facebook or Twitter, so I set out to find the libraries who have made social media a well-supported part of their mission. This led me into conversations with the British Library, the New York Public Library and the Vancouver Public Library, among many others. In some cases, libraries have not just made these a convenient way to distribute information, but have seen their following develop a life of its own.

The Library of Congress started a major trend when it began putting images from its vast collection on Flickr and inviting users to add tags. After the creation of the Creative Commons, a number of the world's top cultural institutions joined suit and added to enriching the online culture. I will show how one public library in Wisconsin used its Flickr activity to gain recognition from the community – right up to the city council. Google has provided us with an option to create a personalized homepage that only we can see. To help populate these pages, Google has opened up its gates to developers and given us tools to devlop our own gadgets and themes without advanced knowledge of coding. As the veteran of more than 300 of these, I will explain how they are created, and demonstrate the extraordinary work that some libraries have done with them. I will also show how libraries can take advantage of a number of other free things such as the Internet Movie Database to enhance their marc records, and Google Analytics to track the ways that the community uses their services. Everyone knows YouTube's reputation for providing silly entertainment, but in our visit to Google's headquarters we were surprised at how seriously it is pursuing an initiative to make it a force for good, useful information in education.

Google Scholar is evolving from a search engine that targets scholarly citations to a provider of scholarly full text information. We interview one of the Google employees who devised this product to find out what is ahead. Blogs have been one of the most adopted forms of online communication by libraries. At Google headquarters, we learned how it is trying to redefine the concept of a blog, and were shown libraries that have done exceptional work with Google. To help promote library projects in Irish history, I learned how to add our material to Google Earth, using KML files. This book covers that process, and shows how to make elaborate multi-part maps in Google Maps. We will also see how one library created a multi-level map of its library using Google Maps. The age of online text began in 1971. I will report on the man who started it all, as well as the days after 2000 when universities began digitizing books and publishing them on the Internet and before Google Books, and what has happened since, including Internet Archive and the Kindle revolution.

In my two most recent positions, I helped set up the next generation of online catalogs. Encore is a *discovery platform*, an attempt to overlay a classically designed online catalog with a more web-intuitive display, with features such as tag clouds and facets to help users narrow down their searches. In this book, we will see how well that is working. Experts are looking at a near-term future where users are more likely to access the Internet from a handheld device than a full service computer. However, a check of the applications stores shows that just a handful of libraries are listed with their own application for checking the catalog, renewing a book and other library functions. Experts will have their say on how this is changing. As Yogi Berra said, "Predictions are hard. Especially about the future." Nonetheless, I will be showing where a number of information science professors and futurists think the library automation world is going. Along the way, we will see some examples of social media applications that have created problems for libraries.

A career that started with shelving fiction books has ended like this. Library automation has been very good to me. In the words of the Grateful Dead, "What a long strange trip it's been."

About the author

Terry Ballard was born in Phoenix, Arizona in 1946, and has worked in libraries since 1966. He graduated from Arizona State University with a bachelor's degree in English in 1968, and a master's degree in Education in 1980. Since getting his master's degree in Library Science from the University of Arizona in 1989, he has worked as a systems librarian in New York and Connecticut, including Adelphi University, St John's University and Quinnipiac University. He has also taught library science at Long Island University and Southern Connecticut State University. He is the author of one previous book, *INNOPAC: A reference guide to the system*, and dozens of articles. In 1993 he won the Computers in Libraries award for article of the year for "Typographical errors in library databases." In 2011 he won the Outstanding Article of the Year award from the Academic Law Libraries Special Interest Section of the American Association of Law Libraries (AALL). That year, his search project DRAGNET won the AALL award for best library publication, nonprint division. He is a frequent speaker at library conferences, including American Library Association and the Third International Conference on the Book. He is currently the Assistant Director of Technical Services for Library Systems at New York Law School in lower Manhattan. Ballard's wife and son are librarians. His hobbies include photography, collecting first editions of

Mark Twain, and New York baseball (both teams). Steve Earle, the Grateful Dead, Chumbawamba, and Philip Glass can be found on his iPod.

Terry Ballard can be contacted at *terryballard@gmail.com*.

1

What does the Internet have to do with my library?

Abstract: This chapter discusses the ways that library automation and the Internet changed the careers of librarians in ways that cannot be reversed. It traces the history of the Internet, starting with the 1960s when it was designed as a method for making sure research institutions could continue to communicate even after a nuclear war. By the late 1980s, the Internet had spread to most educational and research institutions and hypertext markup language (HTML) was a well-known but somewhat niche method of storing data, but only Tim Berners-Lee had the imagination to put the two things together and create an information revolution.

Key words: ARPANET, CSNET, Google, High Performance Computing and Communication Act of 1991, hypertext, Yahoo!

"The future isn't what it used to be."

– Arthur C. Clarke, British science fiction author

A personal journey

When I was young, and until I was in my late 20s, I consumed a steady diet of science fiction. I thrived on stories of mankind conquering Mars, the moons of Jupiter, the weather, and even the stars. I hoped I'd live to see the future where gas powered cars would be replaced by something unimaginably better. I read the great science fiction writers: Heinlein, Clarke and Asimov. I read the near-great: Zelazny, Farmer and Panshin. They all had one thing in common. Nobody predicted what really happened. Nobody imagined that there would be an information revolution equaling or surpassing that of Gutenberg.

The Internet was being created in the late 1960s, about the time that I started working in libraries. Even though I worked in a large, well-funded library, there was no technology beyond the photocopy machine. Ten years after I started, computers began finding their way into libraries, mainly in the form of large mainframe systems that tracked the library's collection. The first literature had already been inputted as computer text and broadcast to a select band of research institutions, but we didn't know that. It would be the early 1990s before we even suspected the magnitude of what was taking place. A decade later, libraries would be hanging on to achieve stability in the midst of what consultant Rick Barry described as far back as 1999 as an information tsunami (Barry, 1999).

A brief history of the Internet

Advanced Research Projects Agency Network (ARPANET) came out of a government agency (ARPA) assigned to investigate advanced technology for the United States military. Since the 1950s, the military had been concerned about the possibility that even a limited nuclear war could destroy all communications inside the country, so ARPA was charged with the task of developing a robust system that could work around any gaps. It was designed to connect the major universities and research institutions in the country. By 1968, they had a design and sent out 140 requests for vendors to construct the system. Most of the vendors thought the idea was preposterous and never bothered to respond.

On 29 October 1969, the first message was sent from UCLA to Stanford. They were trying to send the word "login," but after sending the first two letters, the system crashed. It was restored later in the day, and the entire word was sent. By the end of the year there were four institutional nodes on the network. By the spring of 1970, the network had reached the East Coast. The Internet was born.

In 1971 Ray Tomlinson sent an email message from one terminal to another in the same room. Tomlinson said that the message was forgettable, and he promptly forgot it. In 1973 Norway became the first overseas country to join the network, quickly followed by the UK. In 1983, the government decided that ARPANET had fulfilled its mission for the military – the military then took more than half of the nodes in ARPANET, leading to a period of transition. By this time the Computer Science Network (CSNET) was created for the benefit of computer science departments who did not have the resources to join ARPANET. CSNET was created through a grant from the National Science Foundation (NSF) for an initial three-year period from 1981 to 1984.

One year later, the NSF began a program to give network access to NSF-funded supercomputing centers for researchers at an expanded number of academic settings. Supercomputing centers were set up at Princeton University, the University of California, San Diego, the University of Illinois at Urbana-Champaign, Cornell University, and the Pittsburgh Supercomputing Center, a combined effort of Carnegie Mellon University, the University of Pittsburgh, and Westinghouse.

The National Science Foundation Network was established in 1985 as a way to connect the five supercomputing centers, along with the NSF-funded National Center for Atmospheric Research, to each other and to other educational networks, and then to campus networks all over the country.

Senator Albert Gore Jr, after hearing a 1988 report concerning a National Research Network submitted to Congress by Leonard Kleinrock, Computer Science Professor at UCLA, sponsored the High Performance Computing and Communication Act of 1991. It was passed on 9 December 1991, creating the National Information Infrastructure that Gore called the "information super highway." This bill not only led to greater Internet access for all, but it funded the development of Mosaic, the first generally available World Wide Web browser in 1993.

The World Wide Web

In 1965 Ted Nelson had written about a concept called *hypertext*. This was a plan for making computer information intuitive rather than hierarchical. At the time, there were no computers that could make this a reality, but by the early 1980s people were starting to use hypertext on their personal computers. One of those people was Tim Berners-Lee, a computer scientist at CERN, the European Nuclear Research agency, who invented a program called "Enquire" to manage a database of information he had compiled about the agency. In the ensuing years, he got the idea of expanding this program to include other computers on a network, and, eventually, to become a universal language for sharing information with other computers, no matter what the location or operating system. He was encouraged to submit this idea as a formal proposal to CERN management (Berners-Lee and Fischetti, 1999).

Berners-Lee submitted his proposal in March of 1989, and it sat, unanswered, for more than a year. Eventually, his supervisor gave him the okay to purchase a new computer and try it out. He procured a NeXT computer (a product of Apple co-founder Steve Jobs during his exile from Apple), and got to work. His idea was slow to catch on. First of all, it only ran on NeXT machines in the early days. Secondly, CERN had a specific mission for nuclear research, not information science. Fortunately for Berners-Lee, the idea caught the attention of CERN colleague Robert Cailliau. Cailliau had been at CERN for more than a decade and had a good understanding of how to get things done there. He lined up college interns who could handle the coding details, and helped spread the word within the agency. At this time, hypertext was used in a small community of computer scientists, but only in situations where it helped manage data within a computer. It hadn't occurred to anyone else to combine this method with computer networks.

Berners-Lee was riding a delicate balance. He was promoting this as a way to share files within his institution, while quietly promoting the concept as something that could apply to computers everywhere. If he devoted too much time to the latter, he was afraid that his project would be shut down. He puzzled over what to call this concept, and rejected names such as The Information Matrix (TIM), for fear of being too self-referential to his name. Eventually, he settled on the World Wide Web, and began promoting the concept to Internet user groups. The idea caught on slowly but steadily. Berners-Lee reported that by mid-1991, he could detect between ten and a hundred hits per day.

Berners-Lee compared the growth of the World Wide Web to starting a toboggan – considerable effort by the team at first, followed by gravity kicking in. From that point, the idea caught fire, and the inventor noticed an exponential rise as traffic on the web doubled every few months. In the spring of 1994, Cailliau and Berners-Lee hosted the first World Wide Web conference at CERN. Sessions were packed with people from all nations and all walks of life, united by an enthusiasm for helping to develop this new technology. The feeling was so congenial that someone in the press referred to it as the "Woodstock of the Web." In his closing speech, Berners-Lee defined the ideals of the World Wide Web as a mechanism to provide good information to a fair society, and the points were warmly received.

In the summer of 1994 Berners-Lee left CERN to helm the World Wide Web Foundation – a joint project of CERN and the Massachusetts Institute of Technology. He moved his family to Cambridge, Massachusetts, to begin work. His idea was to help the web continue to grow in the way that he had envisioned in the first place. As we see in the web of today, with mailboxes full of spam and online forums filled with anonymous users exercising their right to express themselves in hate speech, his creation eventually got too big for him to possibly control.

Librarians and the Internet

In 1994, in my capacity as Vice chair and Chair elect of the Nassau County Library Association's Academic Division, I set up a program at the SUNY Farmingdale Campus to demonstrate the reference value of information on the Internet. At the time, the star attraction was a site, reachable by telnet, called YAHOO (for "Yet Another Hierarchical Officious Oracle"). This site was created by Jerry Yang and David Filo, graduate students at Stanford University. In spite of one committee member complaining "Not another Internet program," the session was completely packed, as a series of librarians demonstrated the value of information that they found online.

Months later, I sat with a group of librarians and library school students to get our first look at the web, using the newly released browser MOSAIC. As we started browsing and our screens filled with images of favorite movie stars and music groups, the word that characterized the day was "Wow!" The revolution had arrived, and things would never be the same again. Over the years, some librarians would use the new media to their best advantage, but some library school professors took on a siege mentality, describing the Internet as "Us against them." To be fair, librarians were told to remind users that web search engines only delivered sites that were free anyway, in contrast to the databases provided by the libraries, which tended to be digitized editions of reliable journals.

In the years between 1994 and 2000, a number of search engines appeared to compete with Yahoo! – HotBot, Alta Vista, DogPile and others worked to capture a share of the expanding market for web information. Then one new search engine jumped out of the pack and revolutionized the way we search.

A brief history of Google

Figure 1.1 shows Google as it existed on 2 December 1998.

In the summer of 2005, Larry Page, a prospective student of Stanford, was taking a tour of the San Francisco Bay Area, given by graduate student Sergey Brin. The two did not hit it off immediately, but by the autumn, they were working together on a project called "Backrub." They were not impressed with the way that search engines established relevance. Page invented a system called PageRank that determined the importance of a page by the number of other pages that

Figure 1.1 How Google looked at the beginning

Source: http://web.archive.org/web/19981202230410/http://www.google.com/ (accessed 16 January 2012). © Google, Inc.

linked to it, and even to the pages that linked to the linking pages. Brin, the son of a NASA scientist, worked out the extremely complicated mathematics.

After the team got the resources to trawl the entire web and analyze the results, they realized that they were on to something big. They named it "Google" in honor of "googol," a mathematical term for 10 to the power of 100 (it seems like a manageable number until you learn that there are far fewer subatomic particles in the known universe). For two years, Google existed as a popular site on the Stanford web page. By now, Google was using up so much of the university's network resources that the pair decided that starting a company was their only possible choice. Using a tip from a faculty member, they met Sun co-founder Andy Bechtolsheim at his home, demonstrating the site on a laptop. Bechtolsheim was so impressed that he wrote a check for $100 000. This gave them enough to rent space at a friend's house and hire their first employee. On 4 September, they filed for incorporation in the state of California. *PC Magazine* praised the infant effort for its uncanny ability to get things right, and named it one of the Top 100 Web Sites for 1998 (*PC Magazine*, 1999).

In June 1999, the company announced a $25 million investment from Sequoia Capital. That autumn, Charley Ayers, who had previously spent time working for rock impresario Bill Graham and catering for rock band the Grateful Dead, joined as its first chief. The company also relocated to its current location at the Googleplex in Mountain View, California. By 2002, Google was available in 72 languages, including Japanese, Chinese, and Klingon. Late in 2003, Google Print, later Google Books was announced. In 2005 Google Maps was released, and months later they added satellite imagery. The next year, the *Oxford English Dictionary* added "Google" as a verb. Along the way Google changed the way that people search for information and, arguably changed design.

An uneasy relationship

Google tells us that it wants to organize all of the information in the world and provide it to everybody. Librarians answer: "That's what we've done from the beginning of time." A conflict was bound to ensue. In the end, things will work best if each side does what it does best and takes advantage of what the other side does best. In an ideal world, librarians would not even see Google as "The Other Side."

Conclusion

We have seen how the Internet was invented in the 1960s as a communications tool for research institutions such as major universities and government agencies, and hypertext was postulated during that same period. By the 1980s, the Internet was a thriving communications medium, but was generally unknown outside of the research world. At that time, hypertext was a niche medium for computer scientists.

When Tim Berners-Lee combined the two things, this caused a revolution. The rise of search engines such as Yahoo! and Google gave users such a wealth of data that it led to the false idea that all worthwhile human knowledge was already online. The rise of the World Wide Web has been so steady that librarians tend to forget how much it has changed every aspect of their jobs.

Webliography

A brief history of the Internet:
http://arxiv.org/html/cs.NI/9901011 (accessed 2 March 2012)
Google's company history:
http://www.google.com/about/corporate/company/history.html (accessed 2 March 2012).
The search: How Google and its rivals rewrote the rules of business and transformed our culture:
http://www.rapidleansixsigma.org/The_Search.pdf (accessed 2 March 2012).

References

Barry, R. (1999) *Managing the Transition to the Electronic Workplace while there's Still Time.* The Rick Barry Workshops in association with The Caldeson Consultancy. Available at: *http://caldeson.com/old-site/workshop.html* (accessed 20 February 2012).

Berners-Lee, T. and Fischetti, M. (1999) *Weaving the Web: The original design and ultimate destiny of the World Wide Web by its inventor.* San Francisco: Harper.

PC Magazine (1999) "Top 100 Web Sites: July 1999," *PC Magazine Online.* Available at: *http://web.archive.org/web/1999100910 1757/http://www.zdnet.com/pcmag/special/web100/search2. html* (accessed 11 March 2012).

2

Google Custom Search

Abstract: Librarians at the New York Law School's Mendik Library turned a conference tip about a new Google service into an award-winning collection of search engines. DRAGNET is a Google Custom Search Engine that makes a simultaneous search of 100 recommended free legal websites and brings the results back in less than a second. This chapter shows how the engine is constructed, and how tabbed searching can eliminate a restriction on total hits. It also highlights the work of other librarians in creating search engines to provide focused access to quality websites in areas such as social science, health science and book reviews. It also looks at some of the outstanding uses of Google Custom Search and reports on a trip to the Googleplex to visit the people responsible for it. It also shows how the concept of DRAGNET inspired a search engine company to create a search engine for legal topics. As the DRAGNET project progressed from a possible search widget for Facebook to an award-winning website, this demonstrates how easy it is to become a pioneer on the Internet.

Key words: Custom Search, Custom Search Engine (CSE), DRAGNET, Social Science Data Search, tabbed search categories.

"I know well what I am fleeing from but not what I am in search of."

– Michel de Montaigne, French Renaissance author

A new summer project

In the summer of 2010 we were looking for a good summer project that would enhance the research possibilities for users of the Mendik Library of the New York Law School. I noticed that this library had a detailed structure of web pages that provided links to recommended websites such as those of Oyez, the United Nations, Thomas (the legal database maintained by the United States Government), and many others. While these were all great sites, to use these pages, our patrons needed to go in and out of each one and make individual searches. Wouldn't it be nice to have some kind of federated search that looked up a topic in all of these with one search? Then I remembered something that had been shown to me at a meeting of the American Library Association by Ben Bunnell, a librarian turned Google Books administrator. Google Custom Search allows you to set up your own search engine that only looks at sites that you select. I had set one of these up years ago to search for web pages relating to Irish historical documents, but it was not very effective. It occurred to me that the Irish engine was not useful because I had only chosen a handful of sites. Looking at our web page and the one generated by the Law Library of Congress, Harvard, and others, there was an enormous pool of likely sites to choose from in creating a legal-based custom search.

I decided to put this into practice, and by the time I had entered 20 sites, it was becoming obvious that we were on to something big. The results screens had good information and they continued to appear lightning-fast. Normally the results would appear in less than a second. At this point, the work in progress was shown to the full group of librarians. It was clear that this would be a feature of our main web page, not just a Facebook widget as originally intended, and it would be demonstrated to students at the beginning of the autumn semester, and touted as a major new research tool. In the beginning, the project had a series of prosaic names such as "Mendik Library's Federated Search of Legal Databases," or "Mendik Quick Search." After a spirited exchange of ideas it was decided the "Federated Search" was jargon, but library director Camille Broussard struck gold with the name "Dragnet," because the engine "Drags the Net" for worthwhile legal information (Figure 2.1). I managed to retrofit the name into an acronym by coming up with "Database Resource Access using Google's New Electronic Technologies."

By 30 August when DRAGNET was announced to the world, the engine contained about 80 databases. I wrote about the project to a number of listservs. There was almost no direct response, but our tracking mechanism through statcounter.com told the story of the initial impression.

Figure 2.1 The main screen of DRAGNET

Source: http://www.nyls.edu/library/research_tools_and_sources/dragnet (accessed 16 January 2012) © New York Law School

On the first day nearly a thousand libraries looked at it. Some of the visitors had very impressive dot gov addresses. Over the next week, DRAGNET was a hot topic in the blogosphere and the Tweetosphere. Later that week I heard from Nicholas G. Tomaiuolo, a librarian and writer at Central Connecticut State University who had been doing some work of his own on Google Custom Search. He was helpful in steering us towards a solution to the problem of the 100 hit limit in DRAGNET's results. The answer was to set up tabbed search categories in the coding. To do this, you choose "Refinements" in the control panel.

Nicholas Tomaiuolo (2011) wrote in the online journal *CyberSkeptic's Guide to Internet Research*:

> To test how well the refinements tabs improve search results, I initially performed a broad search for immigration. The results had a decidedly U.S. slant – five of the first ten items returned were from the U.S. Department of Justice, three from MigrationInformation.org, one from the National Council of State Legislatures, and one from the HG Directories. I then selected the "International Law" tab; the results changed with five pages originating at the United Nation's Website, two from MigrationInformation.org (one page commenting on resettling in Nordic countries, and the other on the United Kingdom's reluctance to accept immigrants, which were distinctly different from the two pages from the same Website that were found in the general test search), one from RIO: Reports on International Organizations, one from LLRX.com (law and technology resources for legal professionals), and one oddly irrelevant hit from the about the United Arab Emirates that had no mention of immigration.

After the tabs were set up (Figure 2.2), search results in DRAGNET were displaying up to 500 results in less than a second, and the user could choose a field of specialization for a more refined search, or choose the Recent tab to get up-to-the-minute results.

By the autumn of 2010, DRAGNET had grown to my goal size of 100 sites. We looked for new ways to use this technology, and we didn't have to look far. Since 2009 we had been tracking about 150 law journals that put their current issue and at least some of their archive free online. Since we already had a list of sites and the correct URLs, it was an easy task to create a second DRAGNET search bar to search all of the journals instantly. We then added search tabs for specialized journals such as environmental and international law. We also created a Google Custom Search to find material from the constitutions and established law of the 50 states and the federal government.

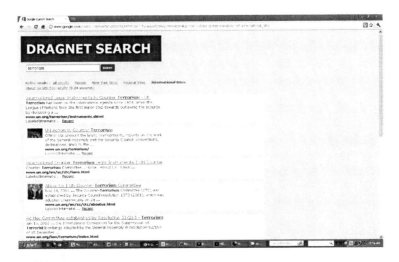

Figure 2.2   Results of a DRAGNET search

Source: http://www.google.com/cse?cx=006465602566811477636:27suauyx5jm
&q=terrorism#gsc.tab=0&gsc.q=terrorism&gsc.ref=international_sites
(accessed 16 January 2012) © New York Law School

In the spring of 2011, we began a project of adding the DRAGNET engines to the iGoogle directory of gadgets. These are all in the directory and accessible to anyone with an iGoogle account (Figure 2.3).

In February 2011, we entered the DRAGNET products in an annual competition to honor the best library publication, non-print division. Early in March, we were notified that we had won. I would be going to Philadelphia in July to accept the award on behalf of the library.

In July 2011, I went to Philadelphia to accept a plaque from the American Association of Law Libraries, along with Associate Library Director Bill Mills. I was also there to present an accepted poster session scheduled for the next day. Also on that day, I was invited to present a series of demonstrations at the "Cool Tools Café," sponsored by the Computer Services Special Interest Section of the organization. I would sit a small number of librarians around a table and show them DRAGNET from the user's point of view and then show them something about how this is all put together. One of the attendees, Connie Crosby was so interested in DRAGNET that she went back to her room and blogged about it that night. She wrote:

Figure 2.3 DRAGNET as an iGoogle gadget

Source: http://www.google.com/ig/directory?q=dragnet&dpos=top&root=%2Fig
(accessed 16 January 2012) © Terry Ballard

> I was particularly impressed by DRAGNET, a legal search tool from the New York Law School demonstrated by Terry Ballard, Assistant Director of Technical Services for Library Systems of Mendik Library. DRAGNET…is a search tool created with Google custom search which we have mentioned a few times over the years here on Slaw.ca. Search results are pulled from 100 "high quality" law-related sites. I was particularly impressed that the search box and results are incorporated into their library resources page.

In a September 2011 visit to the Googleplex, I met with Rajat Mukherjee, the project manager at Google responsible for Custom Search. He was happy with the overall number of customers who used the tool, but unhappy with the lack of imagination that went into much of that usage. I mentioned that most universities just use this to index all of their own pages. He was not aware of DRAGNET or other major Custom Search sites such as Social Science Data Search, so we had a very fruitful and informative session. In October 2011, DRAGNET became available as a mobile phone application. This was part of a package developed for the library by Boopsie.inc., a service that created applications for WorldCat and many other institutions. We had a difficult time adapting DRAGNET for mobile until I heard from Google's Rajat Mukherjee that there was a Google-hosted mobile version of every Custom Search engine we'd created. You just go to a special URL and add the unique ID of your search engine. This guaranteed that there would be uniform display in all mobile platforms. It also limited the number of search results per screen from ten to four.

Also that year, we were contacted by the Chief Executive Officer of Yippy.com, a specialty search engine. He was interested in creating a legal search portal, and was inspired by the way we had invented DRAGNET. It was expected to be released in early 2012 under the name federd.com. Over the

17

past six months, I have been working with the Yippy team and advising them about how the legal portal should look and act.

How it works

To create a Google Custom Search engine, you must have a Google account. DRAGNET was set up within my own account, and eventually I will have to transfer it to an institutional account.

1. Go to *http://www.google.com/cse* to reach the introductory screen (Figure 2.4).

2. Click on the Create button, and a set up screen is displayed (Figure 2.5).

3. Enter the basic facts about your search engine. If you choose the free search engine, you will have ads on your site. However, there is a way to opt out of that if you are working for an educational institution. Just choose the Business settings option on the left, and declare your nonprofit status.

Figure 2.4 Opening screen for creating a Google Custom Search

Source: http://www.google.com/cse/ (accessed 16 January 2012) © Google, Inc

Figure 2.5 Defining what a new Custom Search is about

Source: http://www.google.com/cse/manage/create
(accessed 16 January 2012) © Terry Ballard

After the first few entries, I developed a work flow for adding
new sites. It turned out that not every website works with
Google Custom Search. Ironically, no other Google products
such as Google Scholar or Google Books will create meaningful
results in a Google Custom Search. The way to test these is
to create a second search engine that only searches one site at
a time. One of the features of the custom search engine is a
preview of sites selected. For instance, I would add the URL
for the United Nations and then go to the preview screen and
ask it to search for Ireland. In less than a second, it would
display 100 search results (100 is the limit, but there are ways
around that to be discussed later). Once a site is green-lighted
it is added to the main search engine.

Once you have filled the sites page with your selected URLs,
you may then use the Refinements button to add search tabs
(Figure 2.6). You will be asked to name the search tab and,
optionally, put in typical keywords. More importantly, there
is a setting to emphasize the sites identified with this tab, or
make search results display exclusively from the set. After trial

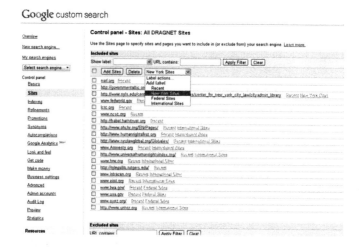

Figure 2.6 Setting up search tabs

Source: http://www.google.com/cse/panel/sites?cx=006465602566811477636: 27suauyx5jm&sig=__scQqYuVf3XwB7TMiwNZoNjNInNk= (accessed 16 January 2012) © Terry Ballard

and error, we found the second option to be superior for our pages. One special refinement we added was a Recent tab that will bring the current year's hits to the top of the screen. We added this thanks to Dave Goessling of the IEEE, who gave me this line of code to add to the "words to search" option:

```
more:recent4
```

In addition, you can add the current year.

Now when you go back to the sites page, you will see a dropdown that allows you to identify each site with one or more of the search tabs.

Other libraries using Custom Search

The most ambitious use of Google Custom Search that I've found is the Social Science Data Search at the University of

California, Berkeley. This was created by Harrison Dekker, and he answered a number of my questions about the project.

I asked him who was responsible for its initial and ongoing selections when it started in 2007. He wrote:

> The project actually evolved from earlier "link gathering" work I'd done using a couple of social bookmarking tools (del.icio.us and connotea). As some point, I decided that search made more sense than tagging, so I added each site to a googlecse. Early on I made a little effort to bring more people into the project, but that didn't gain much traction. In part, that was because a fair amount of tweaking (often involving the use of the cse admin panel) needed to be done to the urls for each added site in order to increase search precision and it seemed non-trivial to come up with an efficient process for vetting site additions. It's much easier to "collaborate" with others by perusing the lists of links they've compiled on their own sites to find candidates for my cse. I've done most of the work myself, but have occasionally used student assistant time to add sites to the cse.

He also wrote that he had no formal program for checking the validity of the links, and that even though he has the site tracked in Google Analytics, he rarely checks for usage.

When asked if he planned to set up another custom search for other areas of the humanities, he wrote:

> No. Eventually I'd like to work on improving my cse, but I'm involved with other projects at the moment. As a data librarian, my main (and almost exclusive) concern is with numeric data. On my campus, numeric data use

in the humanities seems rather small, compared to the sciences. Also, as our library data services program has evolved, there's been an increasing emphasis on services other than "discovery". Not to say we don't offer discovery-related teaching and assistance, but the growth areas seem to be technical assistance (e.g. statistical software), data curation, and collection development.

Brian Herzog is a popular blogger who works in a public library in Massachusetts. He was an early adopter of Custom Search, starting his book review custom search in 2007:

For the book reviews engine, I think it was my friend Kate who originally got me thinking in this direction. She set up a cse to search free academic journals (*http://librarylandadventures.blogspot.com/2007/05/google-is-cool.html* and later *http://librarylandadventures.blogspot.com/2007/10/ive-moved.html*), which might have been the first example I saw of a very targeted use for a cse. Later on, when I realized I was frustrated at work about never being able to find review journals because six of us shared them and someone else was always using the one I wanted, I got the idea to start looking for reviews online. At that time, lots of blogs and 2.0 websites were posting book reviews, and Amazon had a bunch from traditional review sources like Booklist and Publishers Weekly (in addition to customer reviews), so I set up this search engine to solve that problem. I read many more blogs back then than now, so at the time I had a pretty good list of peers or professionals who were doing book reviews – not to mention larger sites like NPR, Slashdot, Bookpage, and sites like Library thing. Also, after I posted about what

I was doing, I got lots of other suggestions. So the initial group of review sites I searched were found that way, and a few more were added over time as I found them.

On a similar note, Christina Crocker of the East Meadow Public Library in Long Island, New York, created GOOD READS to locate readers' advisory material from publishers. The page explains:

> GOOD READS stands for "Google Directory Readers Advisory Search," a specialized search engine that is derived from DRAGNET (Database Retrieval Access using Google's New Electronic Technology), an original concept created by Terry Ballard, Automation Librarian at the New York Law School. A DRAGNET search is like a Google search, except that it runs in only a select group of websites, produced by the organizations and entities listed below. Your search retrieves the top 100 hits, ranked for relevance by Google's search engine. GOOD READS, our version of DRAGNET, has been developed by the Reader Services Department in order to "drag the net" through various reading group related resources. The sites were chosen by the Reader Services Department for their reliability and usefulness. GOOD READS is a great way to begin your search for discussion guides for your reading group.

Ms Crocker wrote this about her experience with GOOD READS:

> I have found it to be very useful and have used it a few times over the past couple of months. When a patron asks for a reading group guide for a particular book,

instead of having to find out who the publisher is to know which site to go to or having to search multiple reading group sites, I just put the title in GOOD READS and voilà, my work is done. A search that used to sometimes take a few minutes is now done in seconds. The reading guides that I need usually appear in the first couple of hits.

Brian Herzog also has created a Google Custom Search for the local history in his town of Chelmsford, Massachusetts. When I asked him about that he wrote:

> The custom search engine for the Chelmsford History Project (*http://www.google.com/support/forum/p/custom search?hl=en*) went more or less the same way as the book review engine. The idea behind that project was to create a single source online to serve as a portal to all things related to the history of Chelmsford. The long-term goal was to create an indexed database of digitized records, but that would take years. So while we worked on that, I creased the cse as a temporary search, and included all of the organizations and resources I could find that had anything available online regarding Chelmsford history – this included the library's main website and Flickr stream, other groups like the Historical Society, churches and some Town websites.

He also commented that it made him sad that Google Custom Search is so low on the radar as libraries rush to take advantage of sites such as Facebook and Twitter. He hoped that my book would help raise awareness about the power of this service.

Looking to the future

During my visit to the Googleplex, Rajat Mukherjee said that Google is working on an important new feature for Custom Search. At the time of writing, it only works on freely accessible databases. They are working to make a custom search that can work with the subscription databases that nearly all libraries provide for their users. This is similar to the paid services known as "Federated Search Engines" that software vendors sell to libraries – usually at substantial cost.

Mukherjee also emphasized that librarians who want to use Custom Search should regularly visit the user forum (*http://www.google.com/support/forum/p/customsearch? hl=en*). In addition, there is a blog that regularly reports on new features (*http://googlecustomsearch.blogspot.com/*).

Conclusion

A case study of the DRAGNET project at the New York Law School shows that the free Google Custom Search can become a powerful research tool when care is given to its design and site selection. Custom search is a way of searching Google but filtering out all but a selected set of websites. With the addition of search tabs, a user can search any topic and get 500 filtered results back in less than one second. Project managers at Google are frustrated with the sort of implementation done by most schools – simply using Custom Search as a way of searching institutional pages. Fortunately, some institutions are going far beyond that – most notably the Social Science Data Search out of the University of California at Berkeley. We showed step-by-step how to create a Custom Search for any specialized area, and we talked with other librarians who have created exemplary search engines.

Webliography

Book Reviews search:
> *http://www.google.com/cse/home?cx=0138406295212052183 40%3Arvfs6n0dgx8* (accessed 2 March 2012).

Chelmsford History Project:
> http://www.chelmsfordhistory.org/ (accessed 2 March 2012).

Connie Crosby's blog about DRAGNET:
> *http://www.slaw.ca/2011/07/25/new-york-law-schools-dragnet-focused-legal-search/* (accessed 2 March 2012).

Consumer Health and Patient Education Information Search Engine:
> *http://davidrothman.net/consumer-health-and-patient-education-information-search-engine/* (accessed 2 March 2012).

Custom Search user forum:
> *http://www.google.com/support/forum/p/customsearch?hl=en* (accessed 2 March 2012).

DRAGNET:
> *http://www.nyls.edu/library/research_tools_and_sources/dragnet1* (accessed 2 March 2012).

Good Reads:
> *http://www.eastmeadow.info/books/goodreads.html* (accessed 2 March 2012).

Law Reviews with online content:
> *http://www.nyls.edu/library/research_tools_and_sources/current_awareness_sources/law_reviews_with_online_content* (accessed 2 March 2012).

Patient handouts at the point of care:
> *http://davidrothman.net/2011/03/18/patient-handouts-at-the-point-of-care/* (accessed 2 March 2012).

Social Science Data Search:
> *http://lib.berkeley.edu/wikis/datalab/Main/GoogleSearch* (accessed 2 March 2012).

References

Tomaiuolo, N. (2011) "DRAGNET: Custom Searching Free Legal Databases," *CyberSkeptic's Guide to Internet Research*, 16(1): 6.

3

Facebook and Twitter

Abstract: This chapter discusses the rise of the major social media sites such as Facebook and Twitter, and shows how libraries of all kinds are using these to tremendous effect. It also introduces some of the newer services such as Tumblr and FourSquare. It shows how major libraries such as the British Library and the New York Public Library became early and enthusiastic adopters of social media, and how they overcame opposition to prove that this was a legitimate way of promoting the institutional mission. It also presents a case study of a small public library in Ohio that made Facebook an integral part of its operation. It uses information gathered at social media conferences to conclude that libraries need to go beyond using social media as a way to send information to their followers. They must find a way to engage these users instead of creating another avenue for top-down communication.

Key words: AdTech, Facebook, FourSquare, SMS, Tumblr, Twitter.

"I was trying to daydream, but my mind kept wandering."

– Steven Wright, American comedian

Introduction

In the 1960s when I first began working in a library, communication between the library and its users was mostly one way. The only exception that I can recall was a wooden box at the circulation desk for people to make suggestions. The suggestions were usually anonymous, so users had no idea if their ideas were being considered until they were implemented. Libraries used the web in the early days as another avenue for putting out their message, but it was still generally one-way communication. With the new online tools of the twenty-first century, this began to change rather dramatically. Users were given the rights in some libraries to add tags to records in the online catalog to enhance searching. They could add their thoughts to blogs generated by the library. They could use FourSquare, a site where people can notify their friends of their current location, to tell their friends that they were studying at the library. For better or worse, libraries' communications with their users was no longer: "We talk, you listen."

A history of Twitter

Twitter's origins lie in a "daylong brainstorming session" held by board members of the podcasting company Odeo. Jack Dorsey introduced the idea of an individual using an SMS service to communicate with a small group. SMS is the communications protocol for sending text in mobile devices. If a message is longer than 160 characters, SMS creates a second file, so Dorsey set up the 140 character limit in Twitter to save 20 characters for file identification. The original name for the service was twttr, later "twitter," meaning "a short burst of inconsequential information," and "chirps from birds."

Twitter began as an in-house communications tool for Odeo employees. The full version was first seen by the public on 15 July 2006. Twitter's popularity was finalized at the 2007 South by Southwest (SXSW) festival. As speakers mentioned it and bloggers in attendance wrote about it, the tweet volume increased from 20 000 to 60 000 per day. The first tweet from space was posted when astronaut T.J. Creamer, with NASA's blessing, tweeted on 22 January 2010.

A history of Facebook

The story begins with Mark Zuckerberg, a sophomore at Harvard, who developed a site called Facemash in October 2003. He posted pictures of co-eds from nine dormitory houses on campus. Zuckerberg obtained the pictures by hacking Harvard's computer networks and copying campus ID photographs. The site was an instant sensation on campus with hundreds of users and thousands of hits. It only last for a few days when the administration shut it down and brought expulsion proceedings against Zuckerberg. The charges were eventually dropped and he went on to a new project of creating an online study guide for art history students that displayed 500 images and allowed students to share notes interactively.

In 2004, Zuckerberg published "the facebook," working with a team of fellow students. In the first month, more than half of the students on campus were registered. By March 2004, the site had expanded to Columbia, Stanford and Yale. Later that year, the company incorporated, moved to Palo Alto, California, attracted investors and bought the name facebook.com. A year later, the company developed Facebook for high school. By September, 2006, membership was open to anyone. The institutional support can have tremendous impact. For instance, the British Museum has an institutionally supported Facebook page liked by more than 150 000 people. In Oxford, the Ashmolean Museum, also one of the world's great museums, has a page that is liked by 2541 people as of this writing.

Institutional presence on Facebook comes in two main flavors. Important museums or organizations that do not want to get involved have a "community" page with information added from Wikipedia. It often happens that the institution adds its official page after a community page has been created, leading to duplication and confusion.

Case study: the British Library

The British Library has a Facebook page that makes it clear that the institution is behind it (Figure 3.1). I made contact with Colin Wight, Senior Content Manager, and asked him

Figure 3.1   The British Library's official Facebook page

Source: http://www.facebook.com/britishlibrary
(accessed 15 November 2011) © The British Library

about the library's experiences with social media:

Ballard: When and how did this get started, and was there substantial opposition from others about taking this path?

Wight: We started with a few podcasts and one or two blogs in 2006, then a Facebook page in January 2008. But it was when we started to integrate social media into our public programmes – Ramayana (2008), Henry VIII and Points of View (2009), Magnificent Maps and Evolving English (2010) – that the benefits became clear: higher attendances at events, hugely increased podcast downloads, new content through crowd-sourcing. Deeper user involvement in general.

Although we knew about Twitter, we weren't convinced that it would be of any great value to us or our users, so it was in February 2009 that we opened an account – more to stop anyone else registering "britishlibrary" than for any better reason. Soon after that Twitter took off, by which time we were experimenting with the Henry VIII exhibition: a joined-up attempt to use "social media" to engage with our web audience, with a blog, Google map, lots of podcasts and videos, Facebook galleries and Twitter feed. I had a very imaginative assistant at that time and we decided we would really go for it and see what worked.

There was no opposition from senior colleagues – probably because our then Director of Strategic Marketing and Communications had a daughter at university who used Facebook, and she encouraged us to check it out. We'd already played around with Second Life and MySpace. Our web team has always been trusted and encouraged to experiment (although we don't claim to have been in the vanguard). No doubt some people were skeptical and will continue to be.

We just pressed on with it in tactical way, assessing progress on a weekly basis. At the same time we came up with draft guidelines for bloggers. Getting these officially agreed has taken a long time, because of the implications of "getting it badly wrong."

As yet we don't have a strategy, other than to increase user involvement and encourage more interest in whatever we do. I am sure that if we had been required to have a signed-off strategy in advance, we would have marked time for a year or longer. In any case I don't think you can easily tell if an organisation has a social media strategy or not! However a strategy is now being considered by our communications team, and that will arrive soon.

Ballard: What sorts of postings did your users respond to the most?

Wight: I suppose this is obvious, but if you post about things that people can actually do, you'll have more success, e.g. visit exhibitions, book tickets for events, download podcasts, "add your voice" (crowd-sourcing using Audioboo) or post photos to a Flickr group.

If I can pick out one activity that was a huge success and would not have worked without

Twitter it's "Map your Voice." As part of our 2010 exhibition "Evolving English" we asked English speakers all over the world to read the same short story and upload it using Audioboo. We then plotted the results on a Google map. The news went viral and we received 1,200 successful submissions, which now forms part of a database for linguists.

Ballard: What kind of workflow is there with these projects? I know that your equivalent personnel at New York Public Library don't have a staff for this.

Wight: The blogs are managed day-to-day by individual curators and other subject specialists with the Web Editor (me) setting them up and offering support such as advice and training. And also monitoring their performance; there are times when you just have to say "this isn't working."

We have arrived at the point where each new temporary exhibition will have a blog written (principally) by the curator, and this is seen as desirable and important part of the marketing and communications activity. It's even enjoyable for the authors. We also encourage guest bloggers from outside the Library.

The main Twitter, Facebook and YouTube accounts are still a "spare time" activity shared between the Web Editor and one or two others in the Public Marketing team. I think that if you have too many editors you lose coherence and a sense of ownership.

The downside is that it has to be supported 7 days a week and in the evenings, to a certain extent. That's not to say 24/7, but it can't be confined to UK standard working hours. That doesn't bother me because as someone with an academic as well as a journalistic background I enjoy these opportunities for self-expression and I like to do a good job.

Maybe soon we will have someone solely employed to look after social media. It's certainly true that we could do a lot more – for example in monitoring other people's blogs and responding to them.

We are now seeing more and more staff wanting to open Twitter accounts: some will find an audience and some will not. It's getting difficult to work out who is talking on behalf of the Library and who is just expressing an opinion. That's going to cause organisations and their employees a lot of angst in the future.

Case study: the Rodman Public Library

Rodman is a small town in Ohio with a population of less than 25 000, but the Facebook page of the Rodman Public Library shows nearly 800 likers. One glance at this page is all it takes to learn that social media is a substantial part of the Library's mission. I had an email conversation with Karen Perone and Amanda Dias from Rodman about their experiences with social media:

Ballard: How and when did you first begin using sites such as Facebook or Flickr? Did the push come from the library director or from the ranks? Was there any opposition?

Dias: The push came from the ranks. I was one of the ones pushing us to be involved in Facebook specifically. I wouldn't say there was much opposition. Many people within the library may not be familiar with Facebook, so it didn't interest some people. But being that I am the one who does most of the administration of the page, it works well.

Perone: We started talking about MySpace first and set up a page geared towards teens in summer 2008. Near the end of 2008, we set up first a Facebook group and then migrated that to a Facebook page as the technology changed. We found the page set up much better for interaction with our fans.

            Flickr followed soon after as an easy way to share photos taken at various library events. This prevented me (the webmaster) from having to do all the complicated tasks involved with editing photos for size and creating web pages for the pictures. The person taking the photos could load them immediately after the program by themselves. Staff was a little hesitant at first to the uploading process, but once they tried it and saw how fast and easy it was, they bought into the new way of doing things.

Ballard: Are there other social media sites that you are thinking of using?

Dias: We use Twitter, Flickr and YouTube. I'm always interested in other sites, checking into new/popular social media sites to see if they would work for us.

Perone: We also have a couple of blogs set up: Computers Can Be Your Friend (*http://www. rodmanlibrary.com/blog/*) set up as a way to "teach" our patrons about computers when we are not offering classes, and, Rodman Recommends (*http://rodmanrecommends. wordpress.com/*) set up to share reviews of library items we are reading. We don't get many (or any) comments on our posts although I think they are read. We have also transferred many of our library website "bookmarks" to Delicious as an attempt to make it easier for staff to assist in updating the listings. I am the only one on staff who knows how to edit web pages and HTML.

Ballard: Do you hear about this from your walk-in patrons and program attendees?

Dias: I haven't specifically heard any walk-in patrons talking about our Facebook page. But we do have 721 fans on Facebook who interact with us online.

Perone: We offer classes on how to use Facebook and usually have a good turnout for them. We also get walk-in patrons to our Open Lab, held on the first Friday of the month, who want some hand-holding on setting up and making their Facebook accounts secure.

Case study: the New York Public Library

I arranged for a meeting with Johannes Neuer, who has the impressive title of eCommunications Manager for the New York Public Library (NYPL).

According to Neuer, social media at NYPL started in the marketing department with Susan Halligan. The initial choice was Twitter in the autumn of 2008. Facebook followed shortly thereafter. Before launch there was an intense planning effort involving the libraries legal team to create social media policies. Encore was being replaced with a discovery platform from Bibliocommons, a company that has also created NYPL's mobile app.

NYPL has created FourSquare sites for all branches, creating virtual badges for frequent users, or "Mayors." It is increasing the local autonomy for branches.

The Library has over 192 000 followers in Twitter, still mainly driven by the Marketing department, which creates a daily tweet on historical fact, and a daily book quote. Traffic has increased by 55 per cent. The Library creates "flagship accounts" for the institution as a whole, and then branches can create their own Facebook and Twitter accounts.

NYPL has also started posting on Tumblr, which Neuer refers to as the most informal of social media sites, and, at the time of the interview, had 10 000 followers. Staff are given training classes in social media. After that, they are allowed to post without further editorial control from above.

By this time of writing, NYPL now has a presence on 2011's exploding social media site Google+.

An academic perspective: Rutgers, The State University of New Jersey

I set up an email interview with Marie Radford, Associate Professor of Library and Information Science in the School of Communication & Information (SC&I) at Rutgers, The State University of New Jersey, and her colleague, Chirag Shah, Assistant Professor in the Department of Library and Information Science.

Ballard: Have you noticed your students having a greater interest in social media in the past 2 years?

Radford: Yes, just last week one of my students asked for more MLIS courses on social media. We presently have one and also social media is integrated into many classes. For example I have a Reference 2.0 and a Management 2.0 assignment for my reference and management classes. Most students, especially younger ones, are avid Facebook users and see social media as venues for library marketing and information literacy instruction.

Shah: Yes. The graduate class on human information behavior that I teach has students in a wide age group, but almost everyone understands and accepts the importance of social media in all branches of personal and professional life. I also teach a freshman undergrad class, in which, no doubt, everyone is on Facebook. Surprisingly (or not surprisingly) nobody in that class uses MySpace, and a very few tweet. In my experience, the choice of and interest in [a] specific social media/networking service does have a correlation with a student's age. Younger students tend to use more YouTube, more features of Facebook, and may not even be on MySpace, whereas older students tend to use more of Twitter and LinkedIn (along [with] Facebook, of course). There is a lot of interest in Google+, but I have yet to see it being used extensively by students.

Ballard: Which social media sites do you believe are the most useful to libraries? Are there new and little-known sites that show promise for library use?

Radford: Right now the mainstream sites seem to be useful – Facebook, Twitter, LibraryThing, blogs. I think Twitter is still being underutilized by libraries and shows promise, although it is not that new. Also, Chirag and I have just written a grant proposal "Cyber Synergy" that will study Social Q&A sites and what lessons virtual reference services could learn/model from these. I'd like to see more shared subject knowledge among librarians who still think of reference in the lone ranger model of one person per question instead of many people answering a question. Our grant announcement is coming out on 9/27 [27 September] so I'll have more to say after that date.

Shah: Definitely the usual suspects – Facebook, Twitter, and YouTube. I have seen several libraries having their presence in SecondLife, but many of them have failed after initial excitement. Nobody in my freshman undergrad class knew about SecondLife, which was sad in a way. I can see Google+ being helpful for connecting patrons to various library services. In addition, iTunes U and other podcasting services are useful for educational uses.

Social Q&A sites could also be very helpful in spreading or supporting library services. Marie and I are involved in a project called "Cyber Synergy," which will look at this possibility. Microsoft has an interesting service under development, called IM-an-Expert, where a chat-based reference interaction is carried out mediated by the system. I can see several such "hybrid" solutions being developed to connect human expertise with machine power.

Ballard: Do you have any other thoughts about libraries and social media?

Shah: I see too many organizations trying to use social media in a wrong way. Just having Facebook, Twitter, and YouTube pages are not enough to have presence in social sphere. One needs to really get their users engaged in discussions and contributions, otherwise these sites are nothing more than more channels of one-way communication. The whole point behind Web 2.0 is to create multi-way communication links for providing community-oriented services. Libraries, and many other knowledge institutions, are often not willing to let go of their "control," creating a mismatch with the social media model. I think there can be a happy medium.

Case study: Reader's Advisory

Alison Kastner (2011) recently wrote in *Library Journal* about a day of Reader's Advisory on Facebook. At the Multnomah County Library they posted the following message: "Looking for a good read? We'd love to help. Send in the last three titles you've read and we'll suggest your next read. Operators are standing by." By the end of the day, they had answered more than 100 queries, and the library saw its most successful Facebook day ever.

Conclusion

Thanks to a generous grant from Yippy.com, I was able to attend the AdTech social media conference at the Javits Center in New York. I heard speeches from Facebook and Google executives, from bloggers, and from Walter Isaacson, author of the new biography of Steve Jobs. At the end of that day I came away with one key concept – institutions must use their social media to engage their viewers and not just use the media as one more way to put out information. As my wife put it – "Publishers get it. One of them put out a Facebook message to write back and tell them what was the first book you really loved as a child. They were bombarded with answers. I felt impelled to send a few in myself. That was successful communication." This concept of engagement is also highlighted in the blog *Forty Cool Ways College Libraries are Leveraging Social Media* (Accredited Online Colleges, n.d.), which shows how some libraries build interest by hosting trivia contests in Facebook or showing books being checked out real time on Twitter.

Webliography

Facebook entry in Wikipedia:
  http://en.wikipedia.org/wiki/Facebook (accessed 2 March 2012).

Twitter entry in Wikipedia:
  http://en.wikipedia.org/wiki/Twitter (accessed 2 March 2012).

References

Accredited Online Colleges (n.d.) *40 Cool Ways College Libraries are Leveraging Social Media.* Available at: *http://www.accreditedonlinecolleges.com/blog/2011/40-cool-ways-college-libraries-are-leveraging-social-media/* (accessed 2 March 2012).

Kastner, A. (2011) "Facebook RA: A day-long experiment spikes user interest, drives readers to great books, and fosters community online," Library Journal, 1 May. Available at: *http://www.libraryjournal.com/lj/community/libraryculture/890008-271/facebook_ra.html.csp* (accessed 2 March 2012).

4

Flickr: if it's good enough for the Library of Congress it's good enough for your library

Abstract: This chapter follows Flickr from its launch in February 2004 to its acquisition a year later by Yahoo! Particular attention is paid to the work of the Library of Congress in using Flickr to display images from its archive and, more importantly, to allow members of the public to tag images for the purpose of enriching the metadata about each image. The Library of Congress pioneers the Flickr Commons, a project to make images available for viewing, tagging and even reuse. This became a rallying point for other major institutions such as the Smithsonian and the New York Public Library (NYPL). We present interviews with the team of librarians who brought the library's Flickr project to life, finding out the advantages and occasional problems with letting viewers add input to their collections. It also presents information about how to set up and enhance a Flickr account, and interviews a librarian in Wisconsin who has made Flickr the crown jewel of his social media efforts. It concludes that this is an effective way for any library to preserve and share images pertaining to their communities.

Key words: Flickr, Flickr Commons, metadata, photo sharing, RSS.

"A true photograph need not be explained, nor can it be contained in words."

– Ansel Adams, American photographer and environmentalist

A history of Flickr

Flickr was launched in February 2004 by Ludicorp, a Canadian company. Founders Stewart Butterfield and Caterina Fake based the service on an online game they had created but not released. The original Flickr was built around an online chat room with real-time photo sharing, but it soon evolved into the sort of site it is today, minus much of the metadata and geotagging data enrichment.

Just over a year after Flickr went live, the company was acquired by Yahoo! for, reportedly, US$35 million. By 2008 the company had lifted any upload limits for paid or Flickr Pro accounts. By 2007, logins and passwords were synchronized to those of Yahoo! The next year, videos were included, but with a limit of 90 seconds (that rule is supposedly still in effect, but I have successfully uploaded videos three to four minutes in length). Particularly since the formation of the Flickr Commons, this has been well-adopted by libraries for hosting their image projects.

Case study: Library of Congress

I spoke with Helena Zinkham and Michelle Springer from the Library of Congress about their experiences with Flickr. They began their project in 2008 by adding two collections to Flickr. "Most people find images on the web – we have to add content on their terms." The library had already done a pilot project of images from the 1930s and 1940s displaying on the library's official website, but the librarians felt that these images weren't getting the attention that they deserved. Flickr makes images more accessible and useful to users. The Library of Congress agreed to sign on to the Web 2.0

approach. They found that this was extremely valuable because users added tags that often contain accurate information to the photos, including the identity of the photographer.

The library got in on the initial phase of Flickr Commons, a home for major institutions such as the NYPL, the Smithsonian Institution and the Irish National Library to share their digital treasures in an environment without copyright restrictions. According to Zinkham, this project makes collections available to a wider audience. They gain new info about the collections, and this increases the visibility of specific photos.

I asked them what the risks of opening up tagging to the public at large are. The answer was that there are sometimes Smart Aleck remarks, although very rarely anything that veers into hate speech, and sometimes loss of meaning because of people swamping photos with tags. On the library's official website, images are available for sale, but the greater access on Flickr has led to reduced revenue from photo sales. Also, the library still has a vast holding of undigitized collections, and these are easily forgotten in the glow of the more public offerings. "Less opportunity for us to have fun as history detectives."

Flickr developed the Commons in response to the needs of the Library of Congress. It was launched in January 2008. In the first 6 months Library of Congress collections got 8 million views and 5000 comments. The most viewed photo has been seen 75 000 times. Library of Congress considers Flickr members valuable volunteers. For instance, a picture labeled something like "Street scene in Akron Ohio," would bring comments from someone who knew the exact address, the year, and the family history of the store owner.

By early 2012, almost 39 000 Flickr members had chosen to make the Library of Congress a "contact," which made the library's images display on their own accounts. That, plus RSS subscriptions, helped to get the word out about the library's ongoing work. The project managers knew that there was much more to this endeavor than high hit counts; it was a good way of alerting management about the value of the operation.

In spite of its exalted status with Flickr, the library still pays $24.95 per year for its Flickr Pro account. At the time

Figure 4.1 Enhanced image from the Library of Congress Civil War collection on Flickr

Source: Image modified by Terry Ballard, hosted at *http://www.flickr.com/ photos/terryballard/6927863074*. Original image at *http://www.flickr.com/ photos/library_of_congress/5228624715*

I interviewed Helena Zinkham and Michelle Springer, they said that they had to patrol comments each day for at least 10 minutes, but abuses were extremely rare. The project has added interactions between citizens and archival staff. The new feature is "Then and Now" pictures.

The librarians told me that because the photographs are published without copyright restrictions, they expect people to take their images and reword them. One of the current collections as of this writing is "Faces of the Civil War," a collection of portraits from the war years – mainly soldiers but some family. I decided to take a few of their photographs and brighten them up a bit in Photoshop, then mount the results in Flickr. Figure 4.1 shows one of the results. The original image can be viewed on Flickr (*http://www.flickr. com/photos/library_of_congress/5228624715/*).

Case study: the Lester Public Library in Two Rivers, Wisconsin

Even though the Library of Congress, NYPL and other top institutions use Flickr to good advantage, there is no rule saying that small public libraries cannot create an outstanding program of their own. When I first started searching Flickr for examples of public libraries using it the Lester Public Library in Two Rivers, Wisconsin kept coming up near the top. I wrote their director, Jeff Dawson, and asked him about his experiences:

> **Ballard:** How did you get started with Flickr and other social media?
>
> **Dawson:** I was hired as director for the Lester Public Library (LPL), Two Rivers, Wisconsin,

March 2007. Prior to this I knew Flickr existed but had not used their services.I owned a digital camera (Olympus C-740 UltraZoom) that I had used a bit only for vacation/dog photos. I have since upgraded my equipment to a Canon XSi with a variety of lenses. I dusted off the camera and started a Flickr account in April 2007, one month after starting as director. I shot photos of our library, photos of books, stacks, posters, programs and anything associated with the library I could think of and posted these photos to Flickr. At this same point in time I felt it important to sign up for as many social networks on behalf of the library as possible for two very important reasons.

1: I wanted to begin branding LPL online and provide as many online access points, beyond our webpage, as possible while holding true meaning and provide fresh information for our immediate community and ultimately, as is the nature with the Internet, the world.

2: There are FOUR Lester Public Libraries in the state of Wisconsin, and I wanted to get LPL Two Rivers branded first and foremost! This was 2007 and MySpace was king and I developed MySpace extensively for several months creating a friend base of over 3,000. I started a blog, "Blogging LPL"; a YouTube account; Twitter and Facebook.There was experimentation with other social media that did not pan out – Beebo and Ning were tried and dropped.

Being a new library director in a new town (Two Rivers, population 12,000), I wanted to raise awareness of the library and myself. I wanted to meet people and become a "fixture" in this small community – truly becoming the "face" of the library. Two Rivers has many events, festivals, and parades, and as part of getting to know the community and people I attended them all. Since I was attending these events anyway, I brought along my camera and took photos and posted those photos to the library's Flickr account; utilizing library philosophy of sharing photos and documenting Two Rivers events. This worked better than I had ever imagined. Because of the library's Flickr account I was interviewed by the local newspaper; our city manager was mentioning the library Flickr account at televised city council meetings and I was interviewed by local radio about Flickr and the other social media I was using to promote the library. By utilizing traditional social media, newspaper, television and radio we were able to promote our online accessibility, our "new" social networking tools. As Chris Peters noted about this interaction, "traditional media outlets and online social media are complementary pieces in a continuous, inclusive public conversation."

By adding the element of documenting not only library events, but community events I was able to further engage my constituency. These photos re-examined the beauty of our unique location for those who lived here but forget what a resource our rivers and lake are. I was able to share back to the community our shared experience of these events. Other entities have noticed – and I was able to go 'deeper' into my community than ever before – and I attribute much of this success to Flickr.

For example, I credit my work in social networking with the following – I sit on the Two Rivers Business Association Board of Directors, I sat on the Manitowoc County Economic Development Corporation Marketing Committee, I presented Facebook for Business and Advanced Facebook for Business for both the Two Rivers Business Association and the Manitowoc Area Chamber of Commerce. I have presented the marketing value of Flickr and other social networks to the Green Bay Chapter of S.C.O.R.E. (Service Corps of Retired Executives). I write a bi-weekly library column for the Manitowoc Herald Times Reporter (our area's daily newspaper). Flickr has put my little library front and center in the library world – I have presented on social networking at the 2008 and 2010 Public Library Association Annual Conferences; presented my social networking experience at the Wisconsin Library Association Annual Conference; presented webinars for Wisconsin Library Systems; presented the topic to the Wisconsin Association of Senior Centers Annual Conference; and presented a webinar for WebJuncition – just to name some of the exposure for my library inside and outside my service area.

With this said, Flickr is my favorite – I have found a talent for taking and manipulating photos, and it remains fun. Flickr is the center of my social network universe – I use photos posted in Flickr in all my other networks, except YouTube. I tend to let the photos do the 'talking' – a photo is worth a thousand words.

Ballard: Have you had response from new patrons coming in and mentioning your online presence?

Dawson: Continually, new and current patrons frequently comment on the photos; Facebook and Twitter accounts. I have had worldwide exposure and my library is popular in Germany, Japan and other European nations.

Ballard: What other social media sites are a part of your operation?

Dawson: Facebook – I co-administer the City of Two Rivers Facebook page and the Two Rivers Business Association Facebook page providing library input and influence across an even wider online audience. With both Flickr and Facebook, I am reconnecting Two Rivers natives who have moved to the four corners of the globe with their home town; this is extremely satisfying.

Twitter, Library Blog, a Teen Blog, Teen Blog – managed by the Youth Services Coordinator, YouTube, LPL Web page – I add this because my staff, before I arrived in Two Rivers, utilized and still utilizes the web page much like a blog, posting important and ever-changing events and notices on the front page.

I constantly monitor what is hot and cold in social media – right now I encourage libraries to participate on Facebook if they currently have no social media in place – it is easy, fun and has all the attributes, such as adding photos and video of other networks.

Ballard: I noticed that the library had local history images on separate web pages.

Dawson: The two projects you refer to are:

World War II Homefront Project – A photographic history of Manitowoc County during World War II, and

Historic Two Rivers Photos – Wentorf Photograph Collection

These digitization projects exist online already; I have promoted both through all my other social networks. There are some copyright issues, particularly with the Homefront project that prohibit me from cross posting in Flickr. It has not occurred to me as a possibility, I may have to consider it for the future. My plan for the Wentorf collection, however, does include side-by-side photo comparisons of "then and now."

How to use Flickr

You can get an account for free at *http://www.flickr.com*. If you already have a Yahoo! account, that will work with Flickr. It is free to try out, but you are limited to 200 images. After that, you will need to buy a Pro account for $24.95. That will get you unlimited usage.

Once you are logged in, you will see an upload link at the top of the screen:

1. Click on the upload link and you are asked to browse for the photos to add. This will usually default to the "My Pictures" section of Windows, or the equivalent in the Macintosh.

2. If you want to upload multiple images in one pass, hold down the Ctrl key and select the images.

3. Choose upload, and the photographs will be processed within a minute or two.

Next it is time to add the metadata, or information about the images.

4. If all of the images in the group you loaded have a common theme, you can add a tag that will be displayed with each picture. Tags are searched in Flickr's directory, so they will help lead people to your work. Putting your first and last name in quotes will allow people to search the directory for your work. You can also create or add to a "set"(clusters maintained by you to keep images together that have similar content) (Figure 4.2).

Figure 4.2   Adding metadata to a Flickr upload

Source: http://www.flickr.com/photos/upload/done/
(accessed 17 January 2012) © Terry Ballard

If you want people to see your pictures, a good option is to join Flickr Groups – thousands of specialty forums within Yahoo! for sharing images. I belong to more than 200 of these, with niche interests like dogs, Ireland, New York, Civil War, and so on. One year I noticed that there was no group for Walden Pond, so I started it myself – it just took about five minutes to fill out information about how I wanted the group to run. After you have joined groups, you can call up any of your photos, choose the "Actions" at the upper left and choose "Add to a group." You will then get a dropdown that displays all of your subscriptions (Figure 4.3).

If the location of your image is an important part of its usefulness, you can use the geotagging feature to display the exact location where it was taken (Figure 4.4):

1. Align the map to the point on earth where you took the picture, and move the placemark to that spot.

2. Once it has landed, Flickr will display a list of likely locations, and allow you to choose the one that is the best match.

Figure 4.3   Adding images to a Flickr group

Source: http://www.flickr.com/photos/terryballard/6256710361/ (accessed 17 January 2012) © Terry Ballard

Source: *http://www.flickr.com/photos/terryballard/6256710361/*
(accessed 17 January 2012) © Terry Ballard

When you are logged into your account and go to *http://www.flickr.com* you will get a screen of information showing activity around your account. On the left you will see the most recent comments about your images. Above that, there is a line graph showing hit counts for the last few weeks. At the bottom of the screen there is a summary of images showing how many are tagged, how many are in a group, and so on. You may follow a hot link to images that are untagged and mass tag similar photos.

Libraries making exemplary use of Flickr

If you want to see the best of the best on Flickr, the starting point is the Flickr Commons, which, as of this writing, lists 56 participating institutions. Ten of these are archives, including the National Archive of the United States. Seventeen participants are in libraries, including the NYPL and the National Library of Ireland.

- The Topeka and Shawnee Public Library in Kansas did a Flickr page called "Call of Duty," saluting Second World War veterans in sculpture, posters, mementos and a reception honoring the surviving veterans (*http://www.flickr.com/photos/topekalibrary/sets/72157628002675813/with/6345833034/*).

- The Reedsburg Public Library in Wisconsin has done considerable work in Flickr sharing its local history collection. There are dozens of sets containing more than 5000 photographs. These include topics such as scout troops, musical theater posters from the 1920s, and pictures of the local brewery (*http://www.flickr.com/photos/reedsburglibrary/*).

- In Upper Arlington, Ohio, they have created a massive program of mounting their local history images on Flickr. Usage of the sets runs into the thousands (*http://www.flickr.com/photos/uaarchives/*).

Conclusion

While there are a number of good photo sharing sites on the Internet (including PBase, Picasa and Webshots), Flickr is the one that has caught on with libraries, and has the most activity in social networking. We saw how the Library of Congress used Flickr to gain exposure for valuable image collections that were underutilized, and how feedback from users led to much richer data. We saw how the Lester Public Library in Two Rivers, Wisconsin made Flickr the key ingredient in its social media program, and how this gained considerable recognition for the library. We learned how to upload pictures and add data to make them accessible to other users. With its ease of use and high visibility, Flickr can be a valuable tool for most libraries.

Webliography

Helena Zinkham and Michelle Springer audio interview about the LOC Flickr project:
http://arttechtonic.wordpress.com/2008/04/20/interview-6-helena-zinkham-and-michelle-springer-library-of-congress flickr-project/ (accessed 2 March 2012).

How to use Flickr video:
http://www.youtube.com/watch?v=3R_MWGFvDEE (accessed 2 March 2012).

Photo of unknown Civil War soldier created by the Library of Congress and enhanced by the author:
http://www.pbase.com/terryballard/image/139752017 (accessed 2 March 2012).

Reedsburg Public Library:
http://www.flickr.com/photos/reedsburglibrary/ (accessed 2 March 2012).

Topeka Library:
http://www.flickr.com/photos/topekalibrary/ 6344683400/in/ set-72157628002675813/ (accessed 2 March 2012).

Upper Arlington, Ohio Public Library:
http://www.flickr.com/photos/uaarchives/ (accessed 2 March 2012).

Wikipedia Entry for Flickr:
http://en.wikipedia.org/wiki/Flickr (accessed 2 March 2012).

5

iGoogle and other useful products

Abstract: This chapter focuses on the world of iGoogle – a free service from Google to allow users to create personalized web presences for their own use. At the beginning of iGoogle the pages had banner theme images at the top. Users, including some libraries, used these for branding, but they were replaced early in 2012. Somewhat more complicated is the iGoogle gadget, which has been used by hundreds of libraries to add things such as search widgets to their online catalogs. The chapter shows you how to create XML files that put your products in the iGoogle directory. The work of a few libraries who have made extra efforts with Google Gadgets are discussed. The chapter ends with a description of free web products with clear applications for libraries, such as Google Analytics, StatCounter, Skype and the Internet Movie Database.

Key words: GIMP Google Analytics, Google Documents, Google Groups, Google Mail, Google Voice, iGoogle Gadgets, Internet Movie Database, LibraryThing, QR codes, Skype, StatCounter.

"A free lunch is only found in mousetraps."

– John Capozzi, American businessman

Google Groups

Google groups are forums hosted by Google as a communications tool for people with specialized interests. Anyone with a Google account can create a group, set the security standards (who can see posts, who can post, and so on) and invite others to join. Numerous librarians have created Google groups around a subject specialty or region, including SABINET, an international forum for librarians and LIBTYPOS, a group that tracks likely errors in online catalogs.

Google Mail

Google Mail was released in 2007 as a free application that provided 1 GB of storage space. For libraries who take the trouble to get an institutional Google account, this can be useful in a number of ways. Gmail now provides more than 7 GB of storage space to more than 100 million users.

At the Mendik Library of New York Law School, librarians were facing a move of all equipment from their old library to the new. They knew that for a period of days there would be no campus email. The electronic services librarian encouraged all librarians to get Gmail accounts and signed them up for an online forum to monitor the situation in the days of no service.

Google Analytics

To start Google Analytics:

1. Log in to your Google account.

2. Go to analytics.google.com and choose sign up. You have to answer a few basic questions about your site – what is it called and what the URL is (Figures 5.1 and 5.2).

3. You are given code similar to that in Figure 5.3. Paste this in to your HTML file, just before </head>.

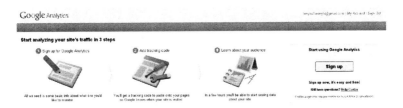

Figure 5.1   Signup screen for Google Analytics

Source: *https://www.google.com/analytics/web/provision#provision/SignUp/* (accessed 17 January 2012) © Google, Inc.

Figure 5.2   Setup screen for a new Google Analytics account

Source: *https://www.google.com/analytics/web/provision#provision/CreateAccount/* (accessed 17 January 2012) © Terry Ballard

2. Paste this code on your site

Copy the following code, then paste it onto every page you want to track immediately before the closing </head> tag.

```
<script type="text/javascript">

var _gaq = _gaq || [];
_gaq.push(['_setAccount', 'UA-27452108-1']);
_gaq.push(['_trackPageview']);

(function() {
  var ga = document.createElement('script'); ga.type = 'text/javascript'; ga.async = true;
  ga.src = ('https:' == document.location.protocol ? 'https://ssl' : 'http://www') + '.google-analytics.com/ga.js';
  var s = document.getElementsByTagName('script')[0]; s.parentNode.insertBefore(ga, s);
})();

</script>
```

Figure 5.3 Code generated by Google Analytics for placement on your page

Source: https://www.google.com/analytics/web/#management/Property/
a28419825w54134773p55032498/%3FpropertyComposite.tabId%3Dtracking
CodeTab/ (accessed 17 January 2012) © Terry Ballard

4. Give it a day for Analytics to locate your page and start logging usage (Figure 5.4).

Figure 5.4 Next day report on traffic from Google Analytics

Source: https://www.google.com/analytics/settings/#scid=18431301
(accessed 17 January 2012) © Terry Ballard

Libraries who purchased Innovative Interfaces Encore platform made significant use of Analytics because the service had no other option for tracking usage. They would sign up as above and the company would embed the code. Using this method at the Mendik Library, there is side-by-side analysis of the discovery catalog and the classic catalog.

iGoogle

iGoogle was launched in 2007, replacing a product called Google Home Page. It is a way to create a personal home page that only you can see – a page that follows you to whatever computer you are at, logged into your Google account. There is always a banner, or *theme* at the top of the page, and a three-column area below to add devices or "gadgets." These gadgets can take the form of weather forecasts, quote of the day sites, games, sticky pads, favorites lists and library catalog search widgets. This page replaces the classic Google search page, but you can toggle between the two in your account settings. iGoogle is a very popular service with millions of subscribers.

Gadgets

Gadgets have been a popular choice for libraries, even though they are clearly more difficult to produce than themes. The biggest problem is that they work with XML, which is a very unforgiving programming language. When I started developing gadgets, there was trial and error, with the latter leading the former by about 20 to 1. Unlike the case of Google's KML programming, the company did put in a simple XML file called "Hello World" to get you started. I will now show you how to create a gadget using XML and get it listed in the directory.

1. From the main iGoogle page, go to Add gadgets. The next screen will show the most popular gadgets. There is a link on the right side to Gadget Dashboard (Figure 5.5).

Figure 5.5 Google Gadgets opening screen

Source: http://www.google.com/ig/directory?dpos=top&root=%2Fig (accessed 17 January 2012) © Google, Inc.

2. At this point you see the gadgets you have created (if any). You now have to choose Docs at the top of the screen to get into the editing area (Figure 5.6).

Figure 5.6 Directory of the author's iGoogle gadgets

Source: http://code.google.com/igoogle/dashboard/?hl=en (accessed 17 January 2012) © Terry Ballard

3. Scroll down until you see the editing area (Figure 5.7).

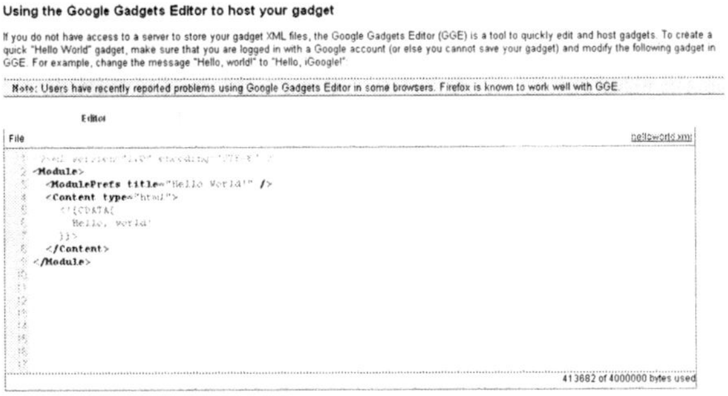
Using the Google Gadgets Editor to host your gadget
If you do not have access to a server to store your gadget XML files, the Google Gadgets Editor (GGE) is a tool to quickly edit and host gadgets. To create a quick "Hello World" gadget, make sure that you are logged in with a Google account (or else you cannot save your gadget) and modify the following gadget in GGE. For example, change the message "Hello, world!" to "Hello, iGoogle!"
Note: Users have recently reported problems using Google Gadgets Editor in some browsers. Firefox is known to work well with GGE.
Editor
File
<Module>
<ModulePrefs title="Hello World" />
<Content type="html">
</Content>
</Module>
413682 of 4000000 bytes used

Figure 5.7 **Google's generic XML file to create a gadget**

Source: *http://code.google.com/apis/igoogle/docs/igoogledevguide.html* (accessed 17 January 2012) © Terry Ballard

The simple file that Google provides shows some of the key structure of a gadget XML file. The problem here is that it is too simple. It is missing fields that would be required in any gadget headed for the directory. The file below has been tested and will result in a workable gadget – just substitute your specific data, and you will produce a gadget that can be added to the directory. Once you do that, open "Hello World," and save as the new name that you choose. Use the file dropdown to save as your file name. You will now see your new name displayed on the upper right side.

4. Click on the name, one of two things will happen:
   - If you get a display with a URL at the top, you are ready to move on.
   - If you get an ugly error message, you need to fix the problem and try again. It is important to know that every time you do this, you must give the file a new name. Also, the author email in this file must match the Gmail account that you are currently using.

Here is the sample file:

```
<Module>
<ModulePrefs title="Your title goes here"
    author="yournametiedtoyourgoogleacco
    unt" height="400"
    thumbnail="http://terryballard.org/
    irelandtn.jpg"
    author_email="terryballard@gmail.com"
    author_link="http://
    googlethisforlibraries.com"/>
/>
<Content type="html">
<![CDATA[
<div style="visibility:visible;width:39
0px;margin:auto;"><embed
    src="http://flash.picturetrail.com/
    pflicks/3/spflick.swf" quality="high"
    FlashVars="ql=2&src1=http://pic70.
    picturetrail.com:80/VOL1882/8512877/
    flicks/1/7465021" wmode="transparent"
    bgcolor="#000000" width="390"
    height="300" name="Acrobat Cube"
    align="middle" allowScriptAccess="sa
    meDomain" style="height:300px;width:
    390px" type="application/x-
    shockwave-flash"></embed></div>
]]>
</Content>
</Module>
```

If the file passes its XML test, you return to the Dashboard and where you find a button at the top called Add a gadget:

5. Paste in the URL when prompted. The gadget will appear on your list of gadgets.
6. Click on the right to add it to the directory. You then go back to your email directory and answer a message confirming your request. After that, it usually takes only a few seconds before it is visible to the world.

In looking at the iGoogle directory, we see that several hundred libraries have created gadgets – most of them search widgets for their online catalog (meaning that thousands of libraries haven't taken advantage of this). At the New York Law School, we also created gadgets to search our popular legal portals using Google Custom Search. However, the most creative use of gadgets from a library that I am aware of is found in the works of Montana State University.

Librarians there have created a gadget that links to their images in Flickr, a Google Map with a tour of the campus, a "Chat with a librarian" gadget, a gadget for displaying videos created by the university, and a gadget that allows you to choose a personalized selection of the databases they provide. Also, there is a news feed gadget and, of course, one that searches the library catalog.

The Combined Arms Research Library in Leavenworth, Kansas has also gone beyond catalog searching and developed a number of iGoogle gadgets for research in military affairs, including gadgets to deliver news feeds and a military Google Custom Search.

Beyond the opportunities for adding content to the directory, there are a number of potentially useful gadgets for ready reference – dictionaries, encyclopedias, weather information and mathematical gadgets.

Google Documents

Using Google Documents is an easy way to do team projects, especially if some of the team members are outside of your institution. It is a suite of products that include word processing, spreadsheets and a presentation program.

Google Voice

Google Voice was launched in March of 2009. It works by giving you a number tied to at least one of your existing telephone accounts. When somebody calls that number, it can cause your mobile phone, work phone and home phone to ring simultaneously, and leave a missed call message in your Gmail account if none of the devices were answered. Before the first year was out, more than a million people subscribed and nearly half of those reported that they used the service seven days a week.

At the 2011 meeting of the American Association of Law Libraries, Karina Condra demonstrated how Google Voice was the communications tool of choice for her library's reference desk. She found its capability of converting a text message from a mobile device into an email message delivered to the account of choice at the desk useful. In other words, it was a single solution for their library's off-site communication with users.

To use Google Voice:

1. Set up your Google Voice account at *https://www.google. com/voice* and choose a Google phone number. You need to provide a working land or mobile number for reference.
2. From your Google Voice account, click on the account settings icon at the top right of the web page settings icons.

3. Select Voice Settings.

4. On the Phones tab, you can choose where to forward calls. If you do not want calls forwarded, just deselect the box next to the phone number. This prevents any spam or wrong numbers going to a landline or mobile phone. However, I have not found spam to be a problem with the Global Spam Filtering options.

5. On the Voicemail & Text tab, choose these:

   - VoiceMail Notifications: Select the box for "Email the message to." The default email is your Gmail account, although you may opt for another account.

   - Text Forwarding: Check the box for "Forward text messages to my email." Make sure the email address listed is the correct account.

Remember to save your changes.

6. Click on the Calls tab for more options, such as spam filtering and caller identification.

StatCounter

StatCounter, a free online visitor statistics tool, was founded in 1999 by Aodhan Cullen, an Irish web designer. To get a page tracked, you have to fill out a simple set of questions, copy code and paste it into an HTML file. Once successfully loaded, the tracking starts immediately. StatCounter reports on the servers and operating systems visitors are coming from, how many times they looked at data in the site, how long they stayed, among many other things. The program is free for a report that shows the most recent 500 visits, and a pay site is available if more data is needed (Figure 5.8).

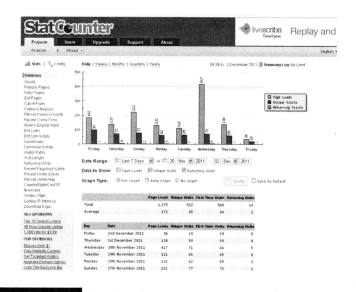

Figure 5.8 StatCounter report of one particular web page

Source: http://statcounter.com/p3085527/visitor/ (accessed 17 January 2012) © Terry Ballard

Skype

Skype is a communications tool to share real-time video conversations through a computer hookup (webcasts). The company has been providing video service since 2006. In 2011, the company was acquired by Microsoft, and it is now a division of Microsoft. Skype is free to operate and use, requiring only a simple camera/microphone device.

Libraries have been using Skype in two major ways that I have noticed:

- For academic library search committees, carrying out interviews over Skype allows them to get a good sense of the qualities and personalities of prospective librarians before they spend money on face-to-face interviews.

- Skype has given public libraries an added dimension – book talks that include a video visit to the author. In the Tuscarawas County Public Library, there were five Skype author events, spread to five separate branch libraries. Skype has created a directory of established authors with fees starting at $100 for a half-hour session (*http://www.skypeauthors.com*).

At the East Meadow Public Library in Long Island, New York, Marcia Blackman, Head Librarian in the Reader Services Department has used Skype several times now in book-related programs. Here are her thoughts:

> Our book discussion group has had extremely successful skyping sessions with authors of the books we have read. The reaction of the group was euphoric. Several members said it was one of the most wonderful experiences they had ever had. As a librarian who has had several interactions with authors through library conferences, I was unprepared for how excited and positive everyone was. The group was equally happy with all authors even though their style and content of books were totally different. Each author was able to have a very meaningful give and take with the group which not only enriched the book but was extremely enjoyable. Lots of laughter, lots of increased understanding of how the author crafts the book and gets his/her point across. It was a win–win situation and you always hope to get those with any presentation. I highly recommend Skyping with authors.

Blackman avoided the Skype author directories and just contacted authors independently.

GIMP (GNU Image Manipulation Program)

On their website (*http://www.gimp.org*), the owners describe their product as a freely distributed piece of software for a variety of tasks in graphics management. Many of the things produced in Adobe Photoshop can be done in GIMP, so this is a good option for small libraries on a budget. Some features are actually superior to Photoshop. For instance, if you are editing a photograph and save it to a different directory, GIMP will take you back to the original directory when you want to edit another photograph. This is said to be the program that Sergey Brin used when he created the first main screen of Google.

IMDB (Internet Movie Database)

The Internet Movie Database (*http://www.imdb.com*) was founded in 1990 by a group of film fans using an online forum of cinema devotees. It was given its current name and URL four years later. While a marc record for a DVD will typically list a film's major stars, producers, director and cinematographer, IMDB gives much richer information about any title. For instance, the entry for *Citizen Kane* gives a plot summary, a detailed synopsis, rankings by readers, and a complete cast and crew list, showing the hundreds of people involved in the film, all the way down to uncredited make up artists (Figure 5.9). All of these names are hot linked so you can see what other films they worked on. Furthermore, there is an FAQ list, user reviews, quotes from the film, links to the trailer, links to Amazon.com to purchase the film in physical or streaming form, data about filming

Figure 5.9 Internet Movie Database screen for *Citizen Kane*

Source: http://www.imdb.com/title/tt0033467/ (accessed 17 January 2012)
© imdb.com

locations, the awards the film has won and more. For libraries to make this available to their users, all they need to do is add a link to the marc record.

Unfortunately, however, most libraries don't seem to do this. I searched the catalogs of 10 big city public libraries for Citizen Kane. Not one of them had a link to IMDB, even though WorldCat shows 15 000 records with an IMDB link. To be fair, quite a few libraries provide links to IMDB as a valued research source, but very few make the marc record connection. Campbell and Fast (2004) think that the format for catalog records is too restrictive, and they call for use of new information technologies in the Semantic Web to provide records that bring in data automatically from the Internet when a record is viewed. They mention IMDB specifically as a high quality source of enrichment information about media products.

The Arnold Bernhard Library in Hamden, Connecticut has added IMDB links to hundreds of their marc records. They have no way of tracking how often these links are used, but given the limited information in a marc record, it is easy to imagine that this would be appealing to their users.

LibraryThing

LibraryThing has an extensive collection of catalog records for nearly any book ever published (Figure 5.10). The site invites users to use this to catalog their home book collection. It has attracted a very large following, and it is full of reader input on nearly any book. After you have added titles from LibraryThing's home libraries, the site will start to report on which users collect the same books that you do. One of the more notable LibraryThing users was the Occupy Wall Street library at Zuccotti Park.

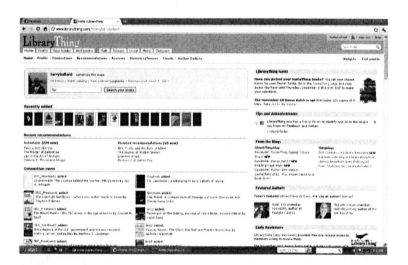

Figure 5.10   LibraryThing personal page

Source: http://www.librarything.com/home/terryballard
(accessed 17 January 2012) © Terry Ballard

KaywaQRcode

QR codes are square shaped barcodes designed for use with smart phones with cameras (Figure 5.11). The user employees a mobile application to align the phone with the square, and this will activate a link to a web page or generate text. Libraries are using this to distribute electronic bibliographies; for instance, in a shelf of light reading, QR codes can be used to display similar titles that may be of interest to the reader. Both functions are available from the KaywaQRcode website (*http//:qrcode.kaywa.com*).

Figure 5.11 A QR code that can be read by a smart phone

Source: http://qrcode.kaywa.com/ (accessed 17 January 2012) © Kaywa.com

Conclusion

We have seen that iGoogle is a particularly popular feature of Google, allowing users to create personalized web pages that can be used on whatever machine they are accessing. Hundreds of libraries have created iGoogle gadgets, but only a few have gone beyond creating search gadgets for their online catalogs, and we have included specific instructions for creating an XML file that can become a working gadget. iGoogle themes are quite underutilized by libraries, but they are easy to create and can be a popular device. Other Google services such as Gmail, Documents, Groups, and Voice have applications for libraries and they are being used. We looked at two of the more popular programs to track web usage – Google Analytics and StatCounter. Skype is a free service that allows users to webcast, and helps libraries interview candidates without travel costs. GIMP is a free graphics program that performs most of the functions of commercial programs, sometimes better. LibraryThing allows people to catalog their personal collections, and it is a good source of information about how books are received by readers. Kaywa provides a free interface to create QR codes, a special form of barcode that can be read by mobile telephone users to get information such as related books or URLs.

Webliography

GIMP (GNU Image Manipulation Program):
  http://www.gimp.org/ (accessed 2 March 2012).
Google Analytics:
  http://analytics.google.com (accessed 2 March 2012).
Google Gadgets:
  http://www.google.com/ig/directory?dpos=top&root=/ig (accessed 2 March 2012).
Google Groups:
  http://groups.google.com (accessed 2 March 2012).
iGoogle:
  http://www.igoogle.com (accessed 2 March 2012).
iGoogle article in Wikipedia:
  http://en.wikipedia.org/wiki/Igoogle (accessed 2 March 2012).
Internet Movie Database:
  http://www.imdb.com (accessed 2 March 2012).

Internet Movie Database article in Wikipedia:
  http://en.wikipedia.org/wiki/Internet_Movie_Database (accessed 2 March 2012).
Kaywa QR code generator:
  http://qrcode.kaywa.com/ (accessed 2 March 2012).
LibraryThing:
  http://www.librarything.com (accessed 2 March 2012).
Montana State University iGoogle Gadgets:
  http://www.google.com/ig/directory?q=%22montana+state+university%22&type=gadgets (accessed 2 March 2012).
Skype:
  http://www.skype.com/intl/en-us/home (accessed 2 March 2012).
Skype Authors:
  http://www.skypeauthors.com/ (accessed 2 March 2012).
StatCounter:
  http://www.statcounter.com (accessed 2 March 2012).

References

Campbell, D.G. and Fast, K.V. (2004) "Academic libraries and the semantic web: What the future may hold for research-supporting library catalogues," *The Journal of Academic Librarianship*, 30(5): 382–90.

6

YouTube: much more than videos of cats playing piano

Abstract: This chapter follows the rise of YouTube from a start up to its acquisition by Google in 1906, and its emergence as a cultural icon of massive proportions. Because of its popularity, YouTube often gets media attention for its more inane content. The chapter details a visit to YouTube's headquarters where a rather different picture emerges. The company is partnering with major universities to add useful intellectual content for people who are self-motivated learners. The chapter also contains detailed instructions for how to upload a video and add useful metadata, including closed caption text and sound tracks from YouTube's vast library of music. It demonstrates how YouTube is used for "Citizen journalism" in cases such as an author who wanted to help save an urban library. In addition, it shows data proving that videos containing distorted information about medical issues can be more popular than truthful ones.

Key words: citizen journalism, closed captioning, YouTube.

"Photography is truth. And cinema is truth twenty-four times a second."

– Jean-Luc Godard, French-Swiss film director

A history of YouTube

YouTube, a video hosting service, was created in February 2005 by three former employees of PayPal, using US$11 million in venture capital from Sequoia Capital (Figure 6.1). From an initial office over a pizza parlor in San Mateo, California, the company now has a permanent three story facility in San Bruno, about twenty miles south of San Francisco. By November of 2006, the company had been bought by Google, Inc., and now is a division of Google.

Figure 6.1   YouTube's initial look, April 2005

Source: http://web.archive.org/web/20050505071842/http://www.youtube.com/ (accessed 17 January 2012) © Google, Inc.

Initially, the great majority of the content was video uploaded by users, but in November 2008, YouTube signed a deal with MGM, Lions Gate Entertainment and CBS allowing the companies to post full-length films and television episodes on the site, with advertisements at the beginning of every video, in a section for US customers.

A visit to YouTube headquarters

On 20 September 2011, we left the Googleplex in Mountain View and made an easy (for northern California) drive down to San Bruno. YouTube is housed in a massive three-story building in an industrial district. We were met there by Jacques Herbert, who works for the educational division of YouTube. Herbert's office is next to a newly installed red carnival slide that allows employees to make a speedy trip to the lower floor. He told us that YouTube had developed a partnership with major universities to deliver video content (Figure 6.2).

Herbert said that more development has gone into the university products because there was resistance to YouTube in the K12 (kindergarten through 12th grade) area. Many K12 schools had banned YouTube, and the company had to guarantee that the educational portal would not allow students to go to the more entertaining areas of YouTube. A quick look at some of the university offerings shows lectures up to two hours long, and the contributors include the Massachusetts Institute of Technology, Harvard, Stanford and the University of California at Berkeley.

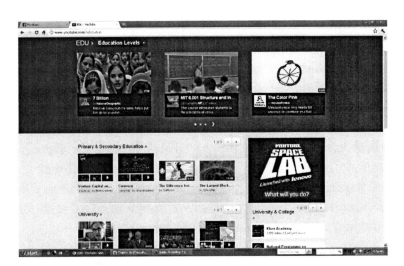

Figure 6.2 YouTube's educational initiative

Source: http://www.youtube.com/education (accessed 17 January 2012) © Google, Inc.

Part of Herbert's educational initiative is YouTube Teachers. This picks topics such as the Berlin Wall or astronomy and provides links to a carefully selected group of the best videos on that topic. Further, as the site explains:

> This site is a resource for educators everywhere to learn how to use YouTube as an educational tool. There are lesson plan suggestions, highlights of great educational content on YouTube, and training on how to film your own educational videos. This site was written by teachers for teachers, and we want to continue that spirit of community-involvement. We're creating a new YouTube newsletter for teachers and are asking teachers to submit their favorite YouTube playlists for us to highlight on YouTube EDU. (YouTube Teachers, n.d.)

Herbert also mentioned the Kahn Academy, which has more than 2700 videos in YouTube. This project grew up out of the author's work in tutoring his nieces and nephews in mathematics. Since they lived in another state, he had to think up some kind of automated solution to get his message across. He started videotaping them, using YouTube as an easy way of getting the lectures to his relatives. Slowly, the word got around as people found them and started sharing them with others. The more feedback he got, the more he lectured. Math is Khan's specialty, and he provides hundreds of lectures on all aspects, from arithmetic to calculus. The lectures tend to be short, anywhere from four to ten minutes, and he provides practice exercises for each topic.

I am a long-time fan of international cinema, so Herbert got my attention when he mentioned that YouTube now has system-generated subtitles. For instance, you can search the French director Jean-Luc Godard and get nearly 4000 hits (Figure 6.3). At the top of the screen on the left, there is a

Figure 6.3   **Searching for subtitled films**

*Source: http://www.youtube.com/results?search_type=edu&search_query=jean
+luc+godard%2C+cc* (accessed 17 January 2012) © Google, Inc.

filter button that allows you to refine a search. One of these
filters is "closed-captioning." Now the results set is about
60, but all of them are labeled "cc." Herbert also led me to
information about how to add subtitles to videos, which
I will share with you later in this chapter.

I also asked Herbert which educational institutions had
done a particularly good job with YouTube and he didn't
hesitate to answer "The Smithsonian." Indeed, the
Smithsonian Institute has done a spectacular job with video.
It has produced hundreds, and the hit count has gone past
1 million. In the featured playlists, the Institute has, for
example, interviews with some of the scientists who work
for it. Its video series on the preservation of world folk
music includes a video of Grateful Dead drummer Mickey
Hart, explaining how he worked with the institute to
preserve native percussion music worldwide.

How to add a video to YouTube

YouTube is compatible with almost any modern digital video camera, and even video smart phones. If you do not already have a YouTube account, it is simple to sign up. If you have a Google account, you can tie your YouTube data into that.

1. At the top of the screen you will see an Upload link. Choose that and use button provided to browse your computer for the file. If your device is connected to your computer through a USB device, you just locate your file and press Enter.

2. YouTube starts processing your file while you add at least some basic information (Figure 6.4).

    At a minimum you need to add a title and description. The privacy level defaults to public. The license defaults

Figure 6.4   Uploading a new video

Source: http://www.youtube.com/my_videos_upload (accessed 17 January 2012) © Google, Inc.

to Standard YouTube, but you can change this to Creative Commons if you don't mind sharing. You must choose a category. These are broad enough that there is never any trouble finding one that works. You don't have to choose tags, but they do help people find your work. In particular, I learned that even though I am the author of a video, my name is not searchable unless I add it to tags.

3. If your video would be more effective with music rather than the original sound, YouTube has provided a vast library of soundtrack music. On the browse screen of your videos, choose Edit Video.

4. When you choose audio, you get access to the library of soundtracks. The first thing you do is to check the box that limits your selection to music tracks that are similar in length to your video. If you have a specific theme in mind you can make a keyword search. Once you have found a likely candidate, you may preview it. If you like what you hear, you may choose to save the new sound. YouTube warns you that this may take some time. Indeed, it can take up to a few hours for the music to arrive.

Adding your own captions

When viewing your list of videos:

1. Choose the Analytics dropdown and select Captions and Subtitles (Figure 6.5).

2. Open the + for Annotations and Captions, and choose a specially designed file from your hard drive. This is a text file with simple information about when to display

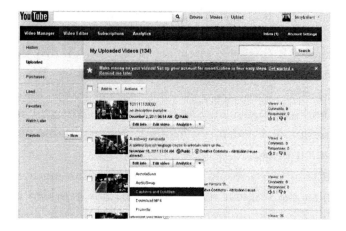

Figure 6.5 Selecting the captions and subtitles work area

Source: http://www.youtube.com/my_videos_timedtext?video_id=kG8C_I9jmGE (accessed 17 January2012) © Terry Ballard

the caption and what to say. Here is an example that you can adapt:

0:00:03.490,0:00:07.430

>> TERRY: All right. So, let's begin.

The dogs are coming around the first turn,

0:00:07.430,0:00:11.600

What happy tails

0:00:11.600,0:00:14.009

Still plenty of walk to go

0:00:14.009,0:00:15.889

This is saved as a text file with the extension .srt

3. Choose the captions and give the file a name (Figure 6.6).
4. Choose Upload File to secure the captions into the video (Figure 6.7).

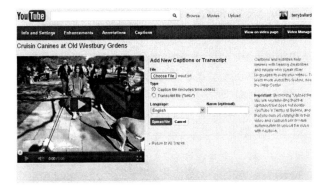

Figure 6.6   Caption work area

Source: *http://www.youtube.com/my_videos_timedtext?video_id=kG8C_l9jmGE* (accessed 17 January 2012) © Terry Ballard

Figure 6.7   A captioned video is born

Source: *http://www.youtube.com/watch?v=FrKGjEd4yq4* (accessed 17 January 2012) © Terry Ballard

Other exemplary sites

At the Copenhagen Business School in Denmark, they have produced a professional-looking guide to the library that has been seen more than 2000 times since 2008.

As of this writing, the New York Public Library has maintained a thriving program of YouTube, with 286 videos, more than 1900 subscribers and more than 800 000 views.

Some of the videos are in niche interests and have modest hit counts, but one that went behind the scenes at the library had thousands of hits. A series of toddler story times taken at various branches had more than 3000 hits per video. The library conducted oral histories of more than a dozen Jazz greats including Marilyn McPartland and Clark Terry. A video of Patti Smith discussing Robert Mapplethorpe had more than 30 000 hits. It seems that the library adds one or two videos per week.

Case study: citizen journalism – Queens Library budget cuts

In the summer of 2010, the Queens Library in New York City was threatened with massive budget cuts and overwhelming layoffs. Some branches would only be open four days a week. This precipitated a major protest at City Hall. I went there with my video camera and took a series of videos of the protesters outside City Hall (outside because they only let them in four at a time). In addition I took a video of my wife reading a message about the library's plight while standing in front of a branch that was closed for renovation. These videos were posted to YouTube, and they caught the attention of my friend Marilyn Johnson, author of the extremely popular book about twenty-first century librarians, *This Book is Overdue!*

Marilyn asked if she could make a video statement to me when we were both attending Book Expo in New York that May. We met up after she had spent an hour autographing audiobooks. She made a passionate plea for library service in Queens that was added to YouTube that night, and generated hundreds of visits. Later in the summer, nearly all of the money was restored to Queens, and they got by with just a few layoffs. I saw Marilyn the next year at the American Library Association, and she told me that she was at a library gathering, and was approached by some administrators from the Queens system: "They told me that my video made a world of difference to their cause."

YouTube can open up possibilities for people like me to practice "Citizen journalism."

YouTube as a source for medical information

Taking on serious topics in YouTube can have a down side. A study published in 2007 by the *Journal of the American Medical Association* (Keelan et al., 2007) looked at the topic of vaccinations on YouTube. Half of the videos were either against immunization or neutral (typically debate formats). The negative videos were found to have unsubstantiated claims, but they consistently had higher hit counts and ratings than the positive videos.

Conclusion

YouTube, a division of Google, is often in the news – usually in ways that emphasize the silliness factor found in some of the contributed material. We have seen the rise of YouTube to a time when the company is providing sophisticated ad-driven copyrighted material. In our visit to the headquarters, we learned that YouTube is involved in a major educational initiative, partnering with a host of research universities to provide educational videos – often of classroom lectures.

We also learned that YouTube provides thousands of lectures from the Kahn Academy – a grassroots effort to give structured lectures on all topics in mathematics and the sciences. However, the populist nature of YouTube means that in showing medical topics there is a danger of misinformation getting through by people with some agenda. We showed step-by-step how to upload a video to YouTube as well as adding extras such as soundtrack and captioning. A look at exemplary YouTube use by libraries proves that the service deserves to be more utilized by libraries.

Webliography

Broadcast yourself on YouTube – really?
> *http://staff.science.uva.nl/~nack/papers/hcc02s-kruitbosch.pdf?q=youtube-broadcast-yourself* (accessed 2 March 2012).

CBS Library video:
> *http://www.youtube.com/watch?v=ppsFW6ECdKc* (accessed 2 March 2012).

Engaging the YouTube Google-eyed generation: Strategies for using Web 2.0 in teaching and learning:
> *http://www.ejel.org/issue/download.html?idArticle=64* (accessed 2 March 2012).

John Palfrey on the Digital Public Library of America:
> *http://www.youtube.com/watch?v=zrmO-qUzjxM* (accessed 2 March 2012).

Seattle Public Library tour:
> *http://www.youtube.com/watch?v=HLugNTpFZ4I* (accessed 2 March 2012).

Statistics and social network of YouTube videos:
> *http://www.mendeley.com/research/how-practical-is-network-coding/#* (accessed 2 March 2012).

Uses of YouTube: Digital literacy and the growth of knowledge:
> *http://courses.gossettphd.org/library/hartley_youtube.pdf* (accessed 2 March 2012).

Virtual tour – Perkins Library, Duke University:
http://www.youtube.com/watch?v=IbECkTKY5-s (accessed 2 March 2012).

Wikipedia entry for YouTube:
http://en.wikipedia.org/wiki/Youtube (accessed 2 March 2012).

YouTube traffic characterization: A view from the edge:
http://dmclab.hanyang.ac.kr/files/courseware/graduate/computer_networks/3.pdf (accessed 2 March 2012).

References

Keelan, J., Pavri-Garcia, V., Tomlinson, G. and Wilson, K. (2007) "YouTube as a Source of Information on Immunization: A Content Analysis," *Journal of the American Medical Association*, 298(21): 2482–4 (doi: 10.1001/jama.298.21.2482).

YouTube Teachers (n.d.) Available at: *http://www.youtube.com/teachers* (accessed 11 March 2012).

7

Google Scholar – just walked down the aisle with WorldCat

Abstract: This chapter tracks the creation and further development of Google Scholar. It shows how the product is changing from a supplier of academic citations to a supplier of full text access to its indexed articles. From a visit to the Googleplex in September 2011, the author reports on a discussion with Scholar co-creator Anurag Acharya, who demonstrated a new product allowing authors to create a profile page to track their citations in an intuitive and graphic manner. Acharya also explains the challenges in working with vendors and libraries to get access information that will open up scholarly information to library users. He reports that both vendors and libraries are reluctant to give out their holdings information and IP ranges, leading to a slowdown of access. In spite of that, it is reported that new vendors are being added to the service at a steady rate.

Key words: link resolvers, OCLC, scholarly publishing, WorldCat.

"Never let school get in the way of your education."

– Mark Twain, American author

A history of Google Scholar

Google Scholar is a freely accessible web search engine that indexes the full text of scholarly literature across an array of publishing formats and disciplines. Google Scholar was created by Alex Verstak and Anurag Acharya, both of whom were then working on building Google's main web index.

The product was released in beta on 20 November 2004 (Figure 7.1). From day 1, its motto has been "Stand on the shoulders of giants." In 2006, citation counting was added to the index. This put it in competition with vendors who sold citation counting databases, usually at very high prices.

In 2007, Acharya announced that Google Scholar had started a program to digitize and host journal articles in cooperation with their publishers, an effort separate from Google Books, whose scans of older journals do not include the metadata required for identifying specific articles in specific issues. This was released in beta on 20 November 2004. The Google Scholar index includes most peer-reviewed online journals of Europe and America's largest scholarly publishers.

Literature about Google Scholar

In 2007, a study was made comparing Google Scholar to Google, Yahoo!, and Ask.com (Robinson and Wusteman, 2007). It found that Google Scholar was the superior product for searching scientific topics, but much less effective in the social sciences and humanities.

Figure 7.1 Google Scholar on opening day

Source: http://web.archive.org/web/20041204051153/http://scholar.google.com/ (accessed 17 January 2012) © Google, Inc.

Case study: Google Scholar in an academic setting

In my years at Quinnipiac University, ending in 2009, we were aware of Google Scholar, but it had almost no impact on the library's work. In the early years, there was little access from Scholar to full text, so we routinely steered users away from it and towards the subscription databases provided by the library. Eventually we heard that Scholar was making more efforts to provide links to subscription services at the library. When I was interviewed at the New York Law School, I was asked what we did about the Google Scholar problem. I asked them to explain. At New York Law School, many students skipped past the online catalog and began their search with Google Scholar. Since the library hadn't joined the Open WorldCat program yet, the links to "nearby libraries owning this work" neglected to mention our library. Eventually New York Law School joined the program and the problem was solved.

Later we noticed that when Scholar was searched on campus there was access to some of the subscription databases, but these were unavailable to users working from home. The library director asked me to look into this problem. To be fully integrated with Google Scholar, a library needed a program called a link resolver, which is a program that takes search results from one site that does not provide full text and finds the same article in another database owned by that institution. Libraries that provide link resolver data and IP ranges to Google can be added as a home library (Figure 7.2), and they would be given the option to search for a given resource at that library. Users can add this to their preferences individually. The Mendik Library did not own a link resolver because all of their databases were already full text.

Figure 7.2 Specifying a home library

Source: http://scholar.google.com/scholar_preferences?hl=en&as_sdt=2,33
(accessed 17 January 2012) © Google, Inc.

In Preferences, we choose a nearby library to track holdings. Now when any of our search results match the holdings at Columbia, we are given a link (Figure 7.3).

Figure 7.3 Search results showing full text availability

Source: http://scholar.google.com/scholar?q=trrorism&hl=en&btnG=Search&as
_sdt=2%2C33 (accessed 17 January 2012) © Google, Inc.

The partial solution turned out to be adding a link to Google Scholar on the library web page that redirected the user to the proxy server. That means that if a user clicks on the link from home, they need to authenticate with their name and school bar code. Then when they search Google Scholar they have increased access to full text articles.

Northwestern University in Chicago enthusiastically joined this program in 2005 after concluding that students were not making enough use of their databases. They not only listed their library, but generated a campus-wide campaign called "Google Gets Brainy" to make sure everyone in the community knew about it. They also sponsored seminars on the best way to use this service. They were hoping to see a 20 per cent rise in links from Google Scholar to their subscription databases. Instead the number was nearly 80 per cent.

Case study: Ohio College Library Consortium

In the 1960s, libraries in Ohio formed a nonprofit consortium to create a computerized common catalog reflecting the holdings of all libraries in the state. The Ohio College Library Consortium (OCLC) was founded in 1967 by Frederick G. Kilgour, who served as president until 1981. After four years of development, the service went into operation. The immediate effect was that libraries could catalog more books with fewer staff. During Kilgour's term, the service was rolled out to other states and eventually to other countries. Later in the 1970s OCLC introduced a system for interlibrary loan, which resulted in millions of transactions. By August 2010, the number of records had grown to 200 million, and the service currently provides location information on 1 billion items.

In August, 2006, WorldCat became a website to freely search the entire holdings of OCLC. Past versions had required a library login and password.

My work with OCLC

In 1983 I had been working at a branch in the Phoenix Public Library system when I was invited to transfer to the main library to work in the catalog department. My main job was to search the OCLC machines for computer records that pertained to the books the library had recently purchased. We added some coding and sent a signal that this was a book that the library owned, indicating a request for catalog cards to be printed. This work was done on bulky dedicated machines. In the ensuing years, these machines were replaced with IBM personal computers – first running files using 5-inch floppy disks, and later on machines with hard drives.

When the first new machine had arrived, my supervisor told me to learn about it to manage the new computers. This led me to become proficient in DOS (Disk Operating System), the program developed for IBM by a new start up company called Microsoft. Soon I was proficient enough to create "batch files," which could perform a series of operations by just pressing one key, potentially saving keystrokes and time. From that time until this, I have tried to learn something new about computers every day. I credit my work with OCLC as being the catalyst for my long career in library automation. This new interest led me to finally get my library degree. In 1990, I landed a job as systems librarian at Adelphi University in Garden City, Long Island.

In 1991, I started a project of rooting out typographical errors from the online catalog. To do this, I found a way to browse the entire keyword index, taking on one letter per day.

To my great surprise, there were some words such as "adminstrative" or "commerical" that showed up in relatively high numbers. In those days, colleges could not see the online catalogs of other institutions. One day I was visiting a nearby university and I tried searching "commercial," and got five times more hits than we had at Adelphi. My hunch had been that this was a universal problem for libraries because they all got the marc records from the same sources. This led to my first national speaking engagement at the Computers in Libraries conference in March 1992. In a packed meeting room I announced that the problem words were not just a problem in my library – they were a problem in everybody's library, and more than a few people gasped. Then they went home to their own libraries to prove me wrong. Unfortunately for them, I was right.

Since WorldCat emerged as a free social media site, I have had many occasions to steer people there who want to know anything about the existence or availability of a book. A relative of mine has been writing books for decades and had a long list of titles, long out of print, that were now available as electronic books. She asked me if there was any way to tell which libraries had purchased the new ebooks. By directing her to WorldCat, I appeared to be some sort of miracle worker because that is exactly the information she needed.

On the other hand, a colleague of mine at the New York Law School asked me if there was any way to find out when a new book was published on a specialized subject such as corporate taxation in the United States. I told her that OCLC should be able to do that, but I didn't see it on the website so I checked with our representatives. They agreed that this would be a worthwhile thing and that it was on their list of things to do someday, but don't expect it any time soon. Three years later, you still couldn't get that information, but the solution came from an unexpected source. Google Books became subject to a Google Alert, and subject heading was one of the possibilities to set up the alert. My colleague told me that she started to get results from the first day.

OCLC's transition to social media

I was fascinated by the process that opened up the vast OCLC database to the public, so I asked Jasmine de Gaia, OCLC Senior Product Manager, End User Services how this came about:

> This was a conscious decision from both upper management and others. Data from the Perceptions Reports and other sources clearly indicated that users were increasingly growing interested in social content and social aspects to library services. As such, active investments in resources and staff were made to help transform WorldCat from a library site to a social media site. Several social components were evaluated, and a roadmap of functionality and deliverables was created. Over time, WorldCat introduced various social tools, such as lists, profiles, reviews, ratings and tags.

> As the social space has evolved, we are beginning to see fewer and fewer distinctions between "social" sites and all sites – that is, there is a current baseline expectation for websites to offer social components, even if the site itself is not focused on pure social interactions. As such, and since libraries themselves are traditionally social, collaborative spaces, it is becoming increasingly important for libraries (and WorldCat) to offer social tools for their users.

In addition to the development of social tools, WorldCat is also highly aware of the fact that in-house development is not the only option. Users will continue to use a variety of different websites, and the most effective solution for increasing the general relevancy of libraries is to not only build social and custom tools inside of platforms like WorldCat, but to also partner with popular and synergistic sites currently on the web. To this end, a key component of the ongoing growth of WorldCat will include strategic partnerships to assist in the transformation from a library utility site to a social media site.

At the Googleplex

In our September 2011 visit to the Googleplex we had the honor of meeting Anurag Acharya, one of the co-developers of Google Scholar (Figure 7.4). He told me that the project was something of an accident that came out of a sabbatical project. Although Google had been acquiring other sites such as Blogger or Picasa, this was the first product to fly under the Google banner that did a different kind of search from querying the entire web.

Figure 7.4 **Anurag Acharya, one of the co-developers of Google Scholar**

Source: http://scholar.google.com/citations?user=nGEWZbkAAAAJ&hl=en (accessed 17 January 2012) © Google, Inc.

When I asked Acharya what was new and exciting at Google Scholar, he told me that they were beta testing a product called Google Scholar Citations that would allow authors of the articles in Google Scholar to track the citation activity for the articles that they had written. As of this writing, the product has now been made available to all authors. To activate it, you have to fill out a form to help identify articles actually written by others who, by coincidence, have the same name. You then have to state which academic institution you are working at, following which you get an email confirmation. Unlike the search result in Google Scholar, this display shows your articles in citation count order. Clicking on that number will show you the articles that cited your work as well as how many times that article was cited. I added a picture and used the option to make my profile publicly available (Figure 7.5).

I asked Acharya if Google Scholar continued to add publications to its index, and he assured me that it was growing at all times. He told me the biggest impediment was

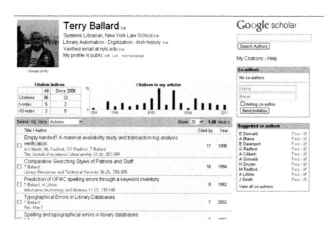

Figure 7.5   New personalized Google Scholar Citations page

Source: http://scholar.google.com/citations?user=UKf7xjEAAAAJ&hl=en (accessed 17 January 2012) © Terry Ballard

that libraries, particularly those in consortia, are jealously guarding information about their IP ranges, and this results in less access for Google Scholar users.

Conclusion

Google Scholar has moved far beyond its original presence as an index to scholarly writing. We expect it to increase its presence as a supplier of full text for serious researchers. OCLC will continue to use its vast network of bibliographic information to pursue new and powerful automation projects. While the service is a main stay for libraries, I expect it to become better known to millions of users in the general public who can use the information that it is providing free of charge.

Webliography

Anurag Acharya helped Google's scholarly leap:
   http://www.indolink.com/SciTech/fr010305-075445.php (accessed 2 March 2012).

Google Scholar:
   http://scholar.google.com (accessed 2 March 2012).

Google Scholar advanced legal research tips:
   http://lawyerist.com/google-scholar-advanced-legal-research-tips/ (accessed 2 March 2012).

Google Scholar article in Wikipedia:
   http://en.wikipedia.org/wiki/Google_scholar (accessed 2 March 2012).

Google Scholar FAQ:
   http://www.library.unlv.edu/help/googlescholar.html (accessed 2 March 2012).

Google Scholar Citations:
  http://scholar.google.com/citations (accessed 2 March 2012).
Social networking and WorldCat:
  *http://www.oclc.org/councils/global/presentations/2009/may/
  Jasmine_DeGaia.pdf* (accessed 2 March 2012).
Using Google Scholar (video):
  http://www.youtube.com/watch?v=bJByIPRrTfE (accessed 2
  March 2012).
What Google Scholar can do for you:
  http://uiuc.libguides.com/gs (accessed 2 March 2012).
WorldCat:
  http://www.worldcat.org (accessed 2 March 2012).

References

Robinson, M.L. and Wusteman, J. (2007) "Putting Google Scholar
    to the test: a preliminary study," *Program: electronic library
    and information systems*, 41(1): 71–80.

8

Blogger: get your message out where the patrons are

Abstract: This chapter shows how Blogger evolved into a useful service with added capabilities such as RSS feeds and podcasting. In a visit to the Googleplex we learn about Dynamic Views, a way to make blogs much more graphic – adding seven new visual templates to the classic blog page. In addition, the Google developers share links to libraries that have done a particularly good job with blogging. We also trace the use of WordPress, an open source blogging product. Both types of blogging tools allow for common elements such as RSS feeds that notify users when a blog has been updated, image uploads, linking and more. We see how a product such as Odiogo can turn a blog into a podcast, to the point of getting it listed in the ITunes store.

Key words: Blogger, weblogs, RSS, WordPress.

"We say little when vanity does not make us speak."

– Francois de La Rochefoucauld

A history of Blogger

Blogger was created by Pyra Labs in 1999. This was one of the earliest weblog programs, and it proved quite popular. Four years later, the company was acquired by Google.

While the original program had a deluxe version that you paid for, Google made all features of Blogger available free. The next year, Google also acquired Picasa, an image hosting program, and integrated it with Blogger. By 2007, Blogger was running entirely on Google servers, and was synchronized with users' other Google accounts. Google added new features into Blogger to mark the company's 10th anniversary celebration, including a new interface for post composition and better image handling.

A history of WordPress

WordPress is a free open source program for creating weblogs, which began as Cafelog, created early in the twenty-first century by Michel Valdrighi. In 2003 WordPress appeared as a joint effort between Matt Mullenweg and Mike Little as an offshoot of Cafelog. In 2004, WordPress got a boost in subscribership when a competing product tightened up its licensing requirements. By 2009, WordPress had grown from a niche product to a powerful presence in open source systems.

A visit with the blog team at Google

One of our later interviews at the Googleplex was with Michael Bolognino, product manager for Blogspot. I was running a bit late, so I had to pack a lot into 20 minutes, but we were quite impressed with his enthusiasm and the ideas he was presenting. He began by saying that, in his opinion, blogs tended to be a bit staid in appearance, and they were working on a major initiative to change this, and that the option was almost ready for general release. It was called

"Dynamic Views," and it would allow blogs to be much more visual. He called up my library blog, librariansonedge. blogspot.com to show me how it would look. There would be six new ways of viewing in addition to the classic look. Figure 8.1 shows the Magazine format.

The most graphic option is the Snapshot view (Figure 8.2).

I asked Michael if there were any libraries that had done a particularly good job with blogs, and he said that the public library in Arlington, Virginia had excelled at creating a blog that looked more like a web page (Figure 8.3).

Figure 8.1   Blogspot Magazine format

Source: http://librariansonedge.blogspot.com (accessed 12 March 2012)
© Terry Ballard

Figure 8.2   Blogspot Snapshot view

Source: http://librariansonedge.blogspot.com (accessed 12 March 2012)
© Terry Ballard

Figure 8.3   Arlington Public Library blog

Source: http://library.arlingtonva.us/2012/02/27/celebrating-the-architecture-of-westover-shirlington (accessed 13 March 2012) © Arlington Public Library

Adding sound

One morning I was in Delicious.com and noticed that one of the most popular bookmarks was concerned with turning your blog into a podcast. That sounded intriguing. A company called Odiogo.com could activate text-to-voice technology to make every blog entry playable, and downloadable to MP3 players and iTunes. The page gave a fairly long list of steps to follow, starting with getting a free account with Odiogo. Unlike most of these accounts, they only wanted two pieces of information – the url of my blog (librariansonedge.blogspot.com) and my email address. Within seconds I was in my blog's Edit mode and they automatically populated it with the code. After five minutes I had "listen to" capability in this blog, an RSS feed to audiocasts and links to MP3 and iTunes.

The voice is vastly better than the famous Steven Hawking computer drone. At its best it sounded to me like a perfectly normal human voice – it reminded me of US Defense Secretary Robert Gates. At its worst it tended to speed up at times. You can help solve the speed problem by adding lots of commas. I think for the most part, it sounded better than I would have. The first time I played it, it helped me to find a typo.

Once the Odiogo account is working on the blog, you can then add the blog to the iTunes store. It took about a day to follow the directions and get approved, but the blog is now present in the store.

Case study: a blog success story

One day, Ian Fairclough, a member of the online forum for librarians working to clean out typographical errors in online catalogs threw out an idea – make a "Typo of the day" to draw attention to the main list of thousands of words at *http://www.terryballard.org/typos/typoscomplete.html*. Within hours, I signed up for a blog, and threw out a rough idea of what this might look at. After enthusiastic responses from key members of the group, we just took that and kept going. You can see the results at *http://librarytypos.blogspot.com/*.

By the middle of the week, Ian had made an announcement of the page in the OCLC listserv, and we began being swamped with people wanting to join the libtypos forum. By the second day of this, someone asked if we had set up an RSS feed. On Blogger's FAQ page there was an entry about RSS. It told me to go to feedburner.com and work with them. Feedburner was very easy to work with. They just wanted to know the address of our blog, and created a page to activate the RSS so anybody could subscribe using whatever program they were signed up with. At last count, the site had been visited more than 300 000 times.

Conclusion

Of all the social media programs, blog creation is the one most adopted by libraries. Bloggers should take care to ensure that the postings are visually appealing and economically written. As in the case of Facebook and Twitter, librarians should use blogs as a way to engage their users rather than just broadcast information. It is very hard to get a following for most blogs, so libraries who choose this should be prepared to promote it using any avenue at their disposal.

Webliography

Aberfoyle Park Campus Resource Centre:
   http://campusrc.edublogs.org/ (accessed 2 March 2012).
Are libraries utilising the full potential of weblogs?
   http://researcharchive.vuw.ac.nz/bitstream/handle/10063/1344/
   thesis.pdf.txt?sequence=5 (accessed 2 March 2012).
Arlington Library blog:
   http://library.arlingtonva.us// (accessed 2 March 2012).
Blogger home page:
   http://www.blogger.com (accessed 2 March 2012).
Blogger article in Wikipedia:
   http://en.wikipedia.org/wiki/Blogger_(service) (accessed 2 March
   2012).
Blogging and uses of blogs in libraries:
   http://shodhganga.inflibnet.ac.in/dxml/bitstream/handle/1944/
   1268/47.pdf?sequence=1 (accessed 2 March 2012).
Blogging for libraries and librarians:
   http://digitalcommons.unl.edu/cgi/viewcontent.cgi?article=1396
   &context=libphilprac&sei-redir=1&referer=http%3A%2F%
   2Fscholar.google.com%2Fscholar%3Fq%3D%2522library
   %2Bweblog%2522%26hl%3Den%26btnG%3DSearch%26
   as_sdt%3D1%252C33#search=%22library%20weblog%22
   (accessed 2 March 2012).

Integrating alumni, librarians and student services colleagues into the intellectual life of the college classroom via Information Technologies:
http://etec.hawaii.edu/proceedings/2010/Fulkerth.pdf (accessed 2 March 2012).

Interview with Michael Bolognino:
https://plus.google.com/102643128217559395667/posts/HMVX xcrX8Gp (accessed 2 March 2012).

Meet your new library website (Arlington, VA):
http://library.arlingtonva.us/2012/02/27/celebrating-the-architecture-of-westover-shirlington/ (accessed 13 April 2012).

Modeling the role of blogging in librarianship:
http://tametheweb.com/wp-content/uploads/2008/10/stephens-mfinal.pdf (accessed 2 March 2012).

Tipperary Library News:
http://www.tipperarylibrarynews.ie/ (accessed 2 March 2012).

The unquiet librarian:
http://theunquietlibrarian.wordpress.com/ (accessed 2 March 2012).

Using new technologies for library instruction in science and engineering – Web 2.0 applications:
http://digitalcommons.unl.edu/cgi/viewcontent.cgi?article=1061 &context=libraryscience&sei-redir=1&referer=http%3A%2F %2Fscholar.google.com%2Fscholar%3Fq%3D%2522library %2Bweblog%2522%26hl%3Den%26btnG%3DSearch%26 as_sdt%3D1%252C33#search=%22library%20weblog%22 (accessed 2 March 2012).

Wordpress article in Wikipedia:
http://en.wikipedia.org/wiki/Wordpress (accessed 2 March 2012).

9

Google Maps and Google Earth

Abstract: This chapter demonstrates the ways that free services such as Google Maps and Google Earth can be used by libraries to highlight their services. It includes a report on how a library in Connecticut added information about its Irish history collections to be viewed in Google Earth. Specific instructions are given for creating this kind of information using KML files, and a sample file that can be adapted to other purposes is supplied. The chapter demonstrates how to make the best use of Google Maps. In a visit to Google's New York offices, new products are demonstrated, such as Google Map Maker, and an Android command to get GPS vocal instruction. The chapter also shows how Google Maps can display images showing a city's evolution over the decades and reports how one librarian in Florida used Google Maps to display floor-by-floor interiors of his library.

Key words: Geotagging, Google Maps, Google Earth, Google Earth Community, Historical Imagery, KML, PDF, XML.

"I'm not sure where we are going, but we're making really good time."

– Yogi Berra, American baseball player

Introduction

In 2003, while working as Automation Librarian for Quinnipiac University, I was sent to Tralee, Ireland to investigate a possible partnership for digitization with the Kerry County Library. The library's local history room was known to house one of the finest collections of Board of Guardians Minute Books in the country. These are the handwritten notes of civic leaders managing the workhouses at the time of the Irish Great Famine. In 2004, the university sent a Minolta scanner with overhead optics to the Tralee library. I was sent to train the Irish partners and begin digitizing. The records from Killarney were chosen, and eventually the images covered a three year period from 1845 to 1848. Later, images from the Kenmare Workhouse were added.

To enhance the presence of these materials on the university website, a new portal was developed in the School of Communications and went live in 2005 as *http://www. thegreathunger.org*. This site displayed links to the Killarney workhouse records. In 2008, the library contracted with CONTENTdm from OCLC to house the most significant portions of its digitization projects.

Geotagging the online collections' locations

The idea for this project started at an American Library Association national meeting in Anaheim in 2008 at a CONTENTdm session that I attended. CONTENTdm is a product of OCLC that provides content management to institutions. The session coordinator mentioned that an academic librarian from Drake University in Iowa found a way to link placemarks on Google Earth and Google Maps back to their university's original content. Since the Arnold Bernhard library had substantial content related to specific geographic locations in New England and Ireland, this seemed like a worthwhile project.

Google Earth is a client-based program that was developed by Keyhole, a corporation that was later bought by Google. Downloads are available at *http://earth.google.com*. It was developed in 2004 and made available as a free download in 2006. It combines satellite images of the entire Earth and combines them, optionally, with numerous layers of value-added information such as roads, geographic boundaries and places of interest. More recently, they allowed users to see what stars were seen above portions of the earth. Users wanting to add photographs to the site can open an account at panoramio.com to add images of specific geographic locations using a simple mapping interface. These images are then evaluated and added to Google Earth if acceptable. The most important rule is the lack of humans in any shot.

Google Maps (*http://maps.google.com*), developed in 2005, is a web-based free service that provides maps for any location in the world. In addition to a map view, it gives an interface to view the chosen location in a web-based satellite image, or to open Google Earth in a machine that has the client loaded.

Existing literature on geotagging

Since Google Earth and Google Maps were so relatively new, there wasn't much to read in library publications. During the early months of this project, several articles appeared. Brenner and Klein (2008) wrote about a similar project, using special programming to get placemarks that led users to their collection of urban planning documents that had been digitized at Portland State Library. Their intention was to use the popularity of Google to increase the visibility of their geographically based online holdings. They also reported that once they started working with KML, the possibilities for new applications appeared in short order.

Jacobsen and Ballard (2008) showed how Google Maps could be used to create useful and attractive online maps that their public library could publish on its web page to better disseminate local information. Jacobsen also noted that few libraries are taking advantage of the powerful free tools provided by Google. In a sidebar to that article, Ballard reported on his discovery of KML applications that linked to Quinnipiac University's original content. Vandenburg (2008) reported on an innovative scheme to create a Google Map that interfaced with the online catalog to show users which books covered particular countries. This approach was later initiated at New York Law School, which created placemarks with further information from the CIA World Fact Book as well as selected photographs of the countries.

Starting the process

I decided to find my way through the tutorials provided by Google. To add a placemark, I had to create KML (Keyhole Markup Language) files, a form of XML. The files would contain a description of the project, a photograph, the coordinates to assign to the placemark, and a link to the university's original content. The problem with the tutorials in Google is that most of them describe much more complicated projects, such as creating an overlay showing all of the crash sites in the Bermuda Triangle.

There is a way to create a placemark inside Google Earth without needing to know any coding, and Google provides a video with precise information about how to make it work. This led me to capture code that started to work in the early KML files. Early on I found that KML files that were also valid XML files would display the lines of code when clicked from of the hard drive. However, if the file is a valid KML file, clicking it will cause Google Earth to be activated, zooming into the location specified in the file, assuming that the coordinates are correct. The default setting for Google Earth is to display the coordinates in the format hours/minutes/seconds. The KML files require numbers in decimal form. You can achieve this by going to Tools/Options and resetting the 3D view to decimal. Once that is done, hovering over any spot on Earth will give coordinates that are an exact match for that site.

Now it was time to let Google know that these files were ready to display. According to the tutorials, you need to go through a five-step process to mount the files on your server, add more files that point to them, and coordinate the effort in your Google Webmaster account (see *http://code.google. com/apis/kml/documentation/kmlSearch.html* for details). After that, wait for a month or two. Instant KML interfaces can be found in Google Maps and Google Earth Gallery. We tried this, and confirmation was displayed that valid files had been recognized. After four months, these files were not seen in the directory of Google Maps or the terrain of Google Earth. The only possible conclusion here is that the system did not work the way Google said it did. One day, months later, I typed my name into a search in Google Gadgets: the search returned icons for the original KMLs that could be added to a Google Desktop as links to Google Maps.

KML interfaces can be found in Google Maps and Google Earth Gallery. The access point in Google Earth Gallery was particularly puzzling. In the page of instructions to developers it says that files must have a correctly formed author field. A subpage about that explains that this entails adding an Atom:Author tag. However, files with such a field are rejected by this interface. Taking out that field gave me a message that the KML was "accepted," but four months later there was no evidence of that.

As described above, there are far too many choices here, and some of them are vastly better than others. I joined a forum for new KML developers run by Google (*http://groups.google.com/group/kml-support?hl=en*). Queries are patrolled by KML experts who always answer promptly. When asked if the placemarks would eventually show up on everyone's Google Earth, the answer was that they would not. It was suggested that the library get an account in the Google Earth Community. If the files were posted there and deemed acceptable, they would automatically display to anyone who had checked Gallery/ Google Earth Community in their Google Earth settings. This was the best advice yet.

The Community exists on two levels. There are two sets of forums based on various topics – one that is moderated and one where anyone can post. On 24 August I posted a message to the open history board about the Killarney project. By attaching the KML file, this automatically generated icons linking to the placemark in Google Earth and Google Maps. Within a half hour, it was found by a moderator and transferred to the moderated section. On the first day, it was seen by more than 100 viewers who were at that site because they had a particular interest in history. This caused an immediate surge in visitors to the library's Irish Great Famine website *http://www.the greathunger.org*. This usage was tracked in StatCounter (*http://www.Statcounter.com*; see Chapter 5).

By late October it was picked up by Google Earth and added to the Gallery layer, eliminating the need to go through the Forum to see it. After the initial success, time was spent fine-tuning the contributions. The volunteer moderators in this community were particularly helpful and knowledgeable (Figure 9.1).

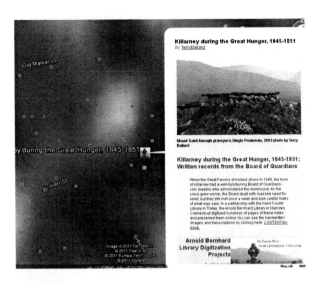

Figure 9.1 KML file displaying on Google Earth

Source: Google Earth (accessed 17 January 2012) © Quinnipiac University

Throughout this process I was looking for a simple template that could be used to create this type of placemark. I never found this, so I developed one myself. To use the template:

1. Copy/paste the coding below into a text editor such as Wordpad.

2. Add your own data and coordinates, and save this as a KML file.

3. If this is present on a machine that has the Google Earth client software, click on the file icon. Google Earth will open and zoom into the destination specified in the file.

Here is the sample file:

```
<kml xmlns="http://earth.google.com/kml/
2.1">
 <Document>
  <name>Yourname.kmz</name>
  <Style id="sh_icon36_copy1">
   <IconStyle>
    <scale>1.1</scale>
       </IconStyle>
   <ListStyle></ListStyle>
  </Style>
    <Style id="sn_icon44_copy1">
     <ListStyle></ListStyle>
  </Style>
  <Placemark>
   <name>What your kml is about</name>
   <description>
<![CDATA[<img src="yourimage.jpg" width=
400>]]><P>Full description of the material
in your placemark http://www.alinktoyour
stuff.org/stuff.html</P></description>
    <LookAt>
    <longitude>120.585493</longitude>
    <latitude>15.167091</latitude>
    <altitude>500</altitude>
       </LookAt>
          <styleUrl>#msn_icon44_copy1
</styleUrl>
    <Point>
    <coordinates>120.585493,15.167091,500
</coordinates>
    </Point>
   </Placemark>
  </Document>
</kml>
```

Working with colleagues I was able to enhance the look of the placemark. By 1 November, I declared that process over because the placemarks now had the look and functionality that I had been seeking.

In November 2008, the single-placemark files that had been created in Google Maps using the simple authoring tool were taken off and combined into larger files that contained information about the library's digitization projects in Connecticut and Ireland. The assumption was that the URLs for these files would be added to the library's web pages as an added discovery tool in accessing the digital collections. Within days we found that these larger files were more likely to generate attention. Hundreds of visits occurred in the first week that these were available. A major improvement in Google Maps arrived late in 2011 when the page for a user generated map provided an option to save the information as a KML file, allowing you to set up links to Google Earth that open in the specified locality.

Google Maps

Later, with an eye to the centennial year of Mark Twain's death, I created a very large Google map of Mark Twain's America, with placemarks for the many places he lived and worked. As of this writing, it has been visited nearly 6073 times, and was a featured link on the very popular blog, Google Maps Mania (*http://googlemapsmania.blogspot. com*). This highlighted a particular problem with the indexing of Google Maps. If you go to Maps and type "Mark Twain's America," you won't find my map. I'm not sure how all of those people ever got there. The problem is that individual map contributors do not get the kind of indexing that institutional contributors get. For a while there was a dropdown in the search bar that allowed you to search user-created maps, but by 2011, that was gone. Lately, I started a quest to have some Twain-related museum "adopt" the map. Late in 2011, I got an email that the Mark Twain House and Museum was interested in doing exactly that.

At the University of Central Florida, librarian Blake Stephens has taken Google Maps and adapted it to create a multi-floor map of the library with tabs giving access to floor plans at each level. His programming is far beyond me, but the details can be found in the "Webliography" below.

At Google's New York headquarters

In October 2011, I visited the New York offices of Google in the Chelsea section of Manhattan. I met with Sean Carlson, Susan Cadrecha and Jesse Friedman. The company inhabits the former warehouse for the New York Port Authority, and it covers an entire city block. As with the Mountain View facility, the place is humming with energetic young people, and snacks are never out of sight. The first thing they showed me was Google's new Historical Imagery. This is a way to look at a city such as London, Berlin, or Las Vegas and see aerial photographs of a particular spot over a 60-year period. Particularly in cities such as Berlin and Warsaw the differences between the 1940s and later were striking.

One site they mentioned was HistoryPin. Google is working with historypin.com, a UK-based web project that encourages users to post collections of historic images and uses geographic data from Google to enrich the experience. This is a fairly new project and the historic collections are provided by a mix of individuals and institutions. In October 2011, the State Library of Connecticut joined the effort. I saw a particularly striking example in a collection of images from the San Francisco earthquake of 1906: a picture with Alamo Square in the foreground, and a city in flames behind. On the side, they added a contemporary shot from the same location.

Conclusion

Google has provided libraries with free tools to enhance the discovery and access to their collections. The simple interface in Google Maps allows librarians to create effective files highlighting important cultural places in their communities. Once librarians get past the learning curve for creating KML files, this opens the door to a universe of possibilities. They should be warned, however, that the world of Google geotagging is filled with contradictory information, and this is a fast-changing environment – what works one day may not work the next. Final placement in Google Earth for items added to Google Earth Community can be uncertain, even when the posting has been added to the moderated lists. The tracking information in Google Earth Community shows that more than 10 000 searches by users with an interest in history have looked at the library's content, so this ended up as a total success story.

Webliography

Connecticut State Library on Historypin:
> *http://cslibweb.wordpress.com/2011/10/27/connecticut-state-library-now-on-historypin/* (accessed 2 March 2012).

Google Earth Wikipedia article:
> *http://en.wikipedia.org/wiki/Google_earth* (accessed 2 March 2012).

Google Maps Wikipedia article:
> *http://en.wikipedia.org/wiki/Google_maps* (accessed 2 March 2012).

Google Maps – You are here:
   http://www.libraryjournal.com/article/CA6602836.html (accessed 2 March 2012).
Historypin.com:
   http://www.historypin.com (accessed 2 March 2012).
ILL Mashup:
   http://www.theshiftedlibrarian.com/archives/2007/01/04/ill_mashup.html (accessed 2 March 2012).
Interactive library map at the University of Florida:
   http://library.ucf.edu/Administration/Maps/ (accessed 2 March 2012).
Library Maps Project by Blake Stephens:
   http://portfolio.resourcefork.com/gallery/librarymaps (accessed 2 March 2012).
Mark Twain's America:
   http://maps.google.com/maps/ms?msid=205472741 11404799 1137.00045dc9dc76fd8686f0a&msa=0 (accessed 2 March 2012).
Moraine Valley Community College map of local interest sites:
   http://www.morainevalley.edu/library/maps/public_libs.htm (accessed 2 March 2012).
University of Central Florida library floor map project:
   http://portfolio.resourcefork.com/ (accessed 2 March 2012).

References

Brenner, M. and Klein, P. (2008) "Discovering the Library with Google Earth," *Information Technology and Libraries*, 27(2): 32–7.

Jacobsen, M. and Ballard, T. (2008) "Google Maps: You Are Here: Using Google Maps to Bring out Your Library's Local Collections," *Library Journal*, 15 October: 26–8.

Vandenburg, M. (2008) "Using Google Maps as an Interface to the Library Catalogue," *Library Hi Tech*, 26(1): 33–40.

10

Electronic books

Abstract: This chapter covers the story of electronic books from "Pioneer times" before Google got into the game and the current world where millions of books are instantly available. Michael Hart, founder of Project Gutenberg and the first person to publish text on the web tells a fascinating tale of the early days. There is an insider look at a grassroots effort at a university to digitize a collection of early works about the Great Famine in Ireland. This illustrates the rise of big operations in digitization such as Google Books and the Internet Archive containing interviews with some of the key people involved. By the year 2000, librarians were hearing that the e-book was dead, as libraries struggled with a number of unsatisfactory e-book readers. Then, in the second half of the decade, the landscape changed dramatically.

Key words: digitization, Google Books, Internet Archive, OCR, Open Library.

"Outside of a dog, a book is man's best friend. Inside of a dog it's too dark to read."

– Groucho Marx, American comedian and film star

Genesis

In the beginning was Project Gutenberg, and that began with the Declaration of Independence. The date was 4 July 1971,

Michael Hart said that he'd been to a fireworks show that evening and didn't feel like going home – opting instead for the computer lab at the University of Illinois, where there was good air conditioning. He had stopped to pick up some food along the way at a small grocery store. This was when America was ramping up for the Bicentennial, and the grocer slipped a reproduction of the Declaration of Independence into his bag. When he got to the computer lab, the paper fell out, and a light clicked in his head. He had been pondering the idea of doing something that would endure on computers forever. He took the Declaration of Independence and began typing it manually on a teletype machine. He said that by the time he finished it was past 1.00 am on 5 July, but he still counts 4 July as the anniversary of e-text. Hart was the undisputed father of e-texts, and he was clearly proud of that. At the time, he wanted to email the file to others on the networks, but learned that this would have taken down the entire Internet – after all, the file was a full 5 KB. They worked out a system so that remote users could ask for a certain nine-track tape to be mounted containing the file, and thus the first Project Gutenberg downloads began.

Hart and I were both on the Book People listserv put out by the University of Pennsylvania – a forum that tracked digitization projects. The previous spring he noticed something that we had done at Quinnipiac University in systematically harvesting Google books and adding the results to our web pages (Ballard and Donnald, 2007). He wrote me that he visited the Hamden area each July, and asked if he could visit and get a look at what we were doing with book digitization. I wrote back and told him that we would be honored if he came by to see our operation.

He was very gregarious and high-energy, passing out DVDs to everyone nearby and giving us permission to copy anything inside and redistribute the texts. We immediately launched into a discussion of baseball after he saw my memorabilia lining the room. I showed him a few of the things we were doing with access to e-books, starting with the work in progress of a graphic interface to electronic reference books, and then the systematic access to Google Books on particular topics. Later, I created a record for him that gave access to a dynamic link of books written by Freud, available in full on Google.

He said that he had a variety of careers between 1971 and the mid-1980s. Among other things, he spent some time in San Francisco as a folk singer – both at restaurants and as a street performer. In the mid-1980s he made another career change when he happened to be running a bicycle repair operation to get money for his bike racing habit. He was called in to tune up a bicycle for a monk who was friends with the new Provost at Benedictine College. The Provost asked him what other skills he had, and Hart mentioned that he could work wonders with computers. Hart built the man a computer that had multiple floppy drives and two hard drives sharing data in such a way that if one broke the other was an automatic backup. This souped-up computing was so impressive to the Provost that he hired Hart as an adjunct professor, and gave him the task of creating the world's first electronic library.

By 1991, when the Internet was starting to become an everyday reality for academics, Hart's library had grown to 10 titles – other government documents such as the Constitution and the Bill of Rights and the Bible. He said the addition of *Alice in Wonderland* "changed everything." "The big difference with Alice was that people of all ages had read it, and kids brought their parents and grandparents to the computer to read it, and vice versa ... it was our first 'big hit,' and I knew from a few events in 1989, prior to the official release, that the whole e-book thing was actually working. People read them, end to end to end, even people I never expected!"

He said that many of the projects that happen in technology are subject to the "S" curve. At the beginning, nobody believes that a project can possibly be done. Then it does happen, and gathers so much momentum that nobody thinks it could ever stop. Then it hits a point where it can no longer sustain the growth and it slows down dramatically. The classic example of this was the "Dot Com Bubble Burst." He quoted an old Chinese proverb: "The person who thinks something cannot be done should not interrupt the person who is doing it."

In the early 1990s, Hart set a goal of 10 000 books freely available online. He attracted enough attention that a volunteer army formed of people who typed public domain works into the computer. Many people said that the goal was unworkable, but he did reach it in 2003. He admitted that he was a workaholic – doing his job until he dropped from exhaustion nearly every day. He said that he had a new goal of a billion books. Yes, a billion. The way this could happen is to take every one of the public domain books on the Internet and translate them into every major language on Earth – 250 languages with at least one million speakers. He asked for guesses what the five most prevalent languages are on the Internet. The first few are easy – English, Chinese, and Spanish. After that it gets rocky – someone correctly guessed Hindi. Hart said "You'll never guess the last one." I chimed in with "Urdu," and to my great surprise, that was correct. He mentioned that in 1998, he was one of *Wired* magazine's "Wired 25." He was flown to Los Angeles and hosted at a red carpet party with the other 24 – including Apple founder Steve Jobs and the man he sat next to, film director Robert Altman.

Hart died in the summer of 2011, but left an unending legacy. By that day, Project Gutenberg contained more than 25 000 titles. I felt privileged spending that day with him.

A university digitization project

In September of 2001 I was inspired by the terrorist attacks on New York City to do something original to help preserve US culture. The library owned a collection of Connecticut history books. Most of these were pre-1923, so the law allowed us to scan them without worry of copyright infringement. I found a large book of the history of the New Haven Colony and digitized it chapter by chapter on the flatbed scanner in my office (Figure 10.1). I learned two things right away. I could make a very attractive and effective electronic book and put it on the web for anyone to visit. However, this was very hard on the book. It was not a coincidence that I chose a book that had a second copy.

The library director was impressed enough that he secured a book-friendly overhead scanner, and gave me a team of student workers to do the scanning. We decided to publish the books in HTML, with illustrations added at the pages where they appeared in the book. Other universities were

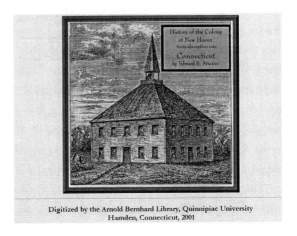

Digitized by the Arnold Bernhard Library, Quinnipiac University
Hamden, Connecticut, 2001

Figure 10.1   Initial digitized title from Quinnipiac University

Source: http://www.quinnipiac.edu/other/ABL/etext/colony/colony.html
(accessed 17 January 2012) © Quinnipiac University

doing projects like this as well, but few of them took the trouble to preserve the illustrations. Most of the books scanned at Quinnipiac were given to the public in HTML format, typically with each file containing a chapter. This got me speculating about adding table of contents information in the marc record to go directly to a particular chapter. I was finally able to do that using a special field in a marc record that could be that specific. This landed me a speaking spot at the Third International Conference on the Book in Oxford, UK. Charles Getchell, our library director, gamely gave me the permission to fly to London.

At that conference, I heard a number of speakers talking about how books and automation should be thought of as sworn enemies. In my presentation, I showed how digitization can bring readers to books that they never could have seen before without traveling hundreds or thousands of miles to a specialized library. The most important speaker at that conference was Ronald Milne, then director of the Bodleian Library at Oxford University, who talked about his commitment to the Google Books project. He showed the group examples of lavishly illustrated books from the late nineteenth century, such as the travel adventure books of Sir Richard Burton. He also said that there were physical problems to solve – particularly in the case of books that had never been read – sometimes the pages were not separated, so they would need to be opened with a razor to read them.

When the Quinnipiac University library opened in 2000 one of the new features was a room devoted to the Irish Great Famine, at the behest of the school's Irish-American president. This consisted of paintings and sculptures commissioned by Quinnipiac, and a collection of books on the topic. We sent word up to the president's office seeking permission to digitize some of these, contingent on absolute guarantees that the books would not be harmed. Permission was granted and we began putting these titles up on the web as well. At that time there were so few digitized titles on the Internet that we became the world's largest supplier of books about the Irish Great Famine at the point of publishing the second title.

Most of the books were of a manageable size, often fewer than 200 pages, but one project turned out to be the signature item of this collection. It was an oversized book called *Ireland in Pictures* by John Finerty, containing more than 400 large landscape pictures of Ireland in the late nineteenth century (Figure 10.2). We then made an HTML file for each image, with navigation at the bottom to go to the previous or next images. The book was artificially divided into eight chapters of 50 images each, and the chapter pages contained thumbnails for image selection (Figures 10.3 and 10.4).

Quinnipiac University had also opened a satellite campus in Tralee in County Kerry. In 2003 I was sent to Tralee for

Figure 10.2 Digitized book of photographs: Finerty's *Ireland in Pictures*, main page

Source: http://www.quinnipiac.edu/other/abl/etext/irish/pictures203/
irelandpictures303.html (accessed 17 January 2012) © Quinnipiac University

Figure 10.3 Subchapters of Finerty's *Ireland in Pictures*

Source: http://www.quinnipiac.edu/other/abl/etext/irish/pictures203/
irelandpicturespart1.html (accessed 17 January 2012) © Quinnipiac University

Figure 10.4 Individual page of Finerty's *Ireland in Pictures* showing navigation options

Source: http://www.quinnipiac.edu/other/abl/etext/irish/pictures203/p11.html
(accessed 17 January 2012) © Quinnipiac University

nearly a month to visit the local history section of the county library and make plans for digitizing original workhouse records with the team there. The plan was to send them a scanner like the one at Quinnipiac and then send me over to set it up and train their staff (Figure 10.5). This was done the following autumn.

Digitizing hand-written records is a different experience from digitizing books. You know that with a book, even a very rare one, there would be other copies left if your library burned down. The minutes of the workhouse managers were an absolutely unique treasure, and adding them to the web gives scholars priceless access. My wife helped me by turning pages in the last round of digitizing – in this case the workhouse papers from Kenmare, south of Killarney. As the famine began to unfold in that town, she couldn't help noticing the tone of panic in the weekly reports, and even saw that the handwriting was becoming less legible. Some of the work we did can be seen on the web (*http://www. thegreathunger.org*). In a long career in libraries, I would point to this project as my greatest source of satisfaction.

During this period, Quinnipiac University and other digitizing institutions reported their latest publications to the University of Pennsylvania, which maintained a master list of

Figure 10.5 The digitizing team at the Kerry County Library

Source: *http://web.archive.org/web/20080211102714im_/http://faculty. quinnipiac.edu/libraries/tballard/scan%20crew.jpg* (accessed 17 January 2012) © Terry Ballard

titles available through Project Gutenberg and the relatively small field of university contributors. Although Shakespeare and all of the major classics were there, the total listing was still only in the thousands. Something was about to happen that would totally change the landscape of electronic publishing.

Google Books

In 2002 a select group of employees at Google began to envision the books project. Their mission was to figure out how long it would take to scan every book in the world, but nobody knew the answer because nobody else had dreamed of such a thing. Larry Page decided to run an experiment on his own. Using the scanner in his office, he scanned a 300-page book in 40 minutes.

Page approached his alma mater, the University of Michigan, which had hosted digital initiatives such as JSTOR and Making of America. At the rate that they were scanning, they estimated it would take 1000 years to scan every book ever printed. Page knew he could make things happen much faster. The Google team developed their own high-speed scanner, which was far more book-friendly than other scanners commercially available. Another group was solving the problem of OCR (optical character recognition) in hundreds of languages.

The team visited the renowned Bodleian Library, where they found the administration to be very receptive. Follow-up meetings and discussions resulted in an agreement to digitize the library's collection of more than 1 million nineteenth-century public domain books within three years. Because copyright is more restrictive in the UK than it is in the United States, the cut-off date for scanning was 1890.

Next the Google Print team began talks with major publishers at the Frankfurt Book Fair, after Page and Brin announced Google Print to the world. Blackwell, Cambridge University Press, the University of Chicago Press, Houghton Mifflin, Hyperion, McGraw-Hill, Oxford University Press, Pearson, Penguin, Perseus, Princeton University Press, Springer, Taylor & Francis, Thomson Delmar and Warner Books all signaled that they were on board. Late in 2004, Google announced the Google Print Library Project, containing partnerships with Harvard, the University of Michigan, the New York Public Library, Oxford and Stanford, for a total of 15 million volumes.

In 2006 Google donated $3 million to the Library of Congress to help build the World Digital Library, designed to provide online access to a collection of rare and unique items from all around the world. They also began digitizing works of historical value from the Law Library of Congress. Google Print had now been renamed Google Books. Soon they had set up an option with their publisher partners to sell electronic access to their books online.

Also in 2006 Google created NGram, a program that tracks the way words are used over a period of time. This is a gold mine for linguistics researchers. To test this out, I used a statement by author Shelby Foote that one major results of the Civil War was the way people wrote the name "United States." Before the war, the common phrase was "The United States are..." After the war, it became "The United States is..." (see Figure 10.6).

As the years progressed, Google added a number of features to enrich the data for the collection. There was integration with Google Maps to show the locations mentioned in a book, but this was sometimes problematic, as names of historical figures such as Saint Augustine could lead to a link for a city in Florida. Later in 2007, Google added an option to view a book in plain text if it was in the public domain – this was a major step forward because the text could be sent to programs that would read the book to vision-impaired users.

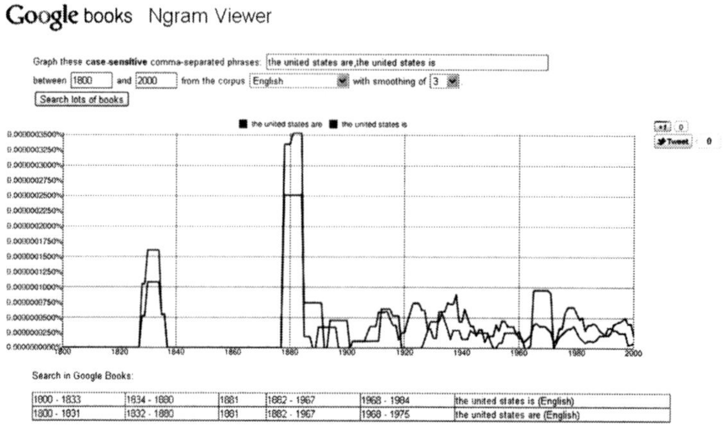

Google books Ngram Viewer

Figure 10.6 NGram shows how word usage has changed over the centuries, confirming Foote's premise

Source: http://books.google.com/ngrams/graph?content=racist%2C++++preudi ced&year_start=1776&year_end=2000&corpus=0&smoothing=3 (accessed 17 January 2012) © Google, Inc.

In 2010 Google announced its estimate that there are about 130 million unique books in the world, and that it plans to scan all of them by the end of the decade. Late in 2010 Google announced that the number of books in its database is over 15 million. As of the writing, that is still the official count.

The Google Book settlement

In late 2005 the law suits began. The Authors Guild of America and Association of American Publishers sued Google in separate law suits. They claimed that the project involved "massive copyright infringement." Google claimed its work was "fair use," and was the equivalent of a highly accurate library card catalog that indexed every word in a book. The Authors Guild vs. Google case never went to court because the two sides went to work finding common ground.

The Authors Guild, the publishing industry and Google announced a settlement on 28 October 2008. Google agreed to pay a total of $125 million to authors of scanned books, to pay legal costs and to create a Book Rights Registry. Harvard Library was unhappy with the arrangement and withdrew its partnership. Google's Book Settlement website debuted on 11 February 2009.

On 22 March 2011, US Circuit Judge Denny Chin of New York rejected the settlement. Chin wrote:

> While the digitization of books and the creation of a universal digital library would benefit many, the ASA [amended settlement agreement] would simply go too far. It would permit this class action which was brought against defendant Google Inc. ("Google") to challenge its scanning of books and display of "snippets" for on-line searching – to implement a forward-looking business arrangement that would grant Google significant rights to exploit entire books, without permission of the copyright owners. Indeed, the ASA would give Google a significant advantage over competitors, rewarding it for engaging in wholesale copying of copyrighted works without permission, while releasing claims well beyond those presented in the case. Accordingly, and for the reasons more fully discussed below, the motion for final approval of the ASA is denied. (quoted in Grimmelmann, 2009).

James Grimmelmann

One of the world's leading authorities on the Google Book settlement is Professor James Grimmelmann of the New York Law School and a valued colleague of mine. One day in September 2011 we met for lunch and I asked him if the appeals in the settlement would go on forever. He told me that a further ruling in a southern circuit court put the final gravestone on Google's plan to provide information from copyrighted works unless the author opted out. The court ruled that it was impossible to determine of the profit splits are fair to the copyright holders. He said that Google should give up on the idea of automatic opt in and work with the things they can do, such as getting authors to voluntarily opt in so that Google can give users previews of their books. The company has a thriving business of selling electronic books for the publishers who did opt into the program. He also said that they have a great opportunity to tie Google Books in with other popular services such as Google+.

Dr Grimmelmann told me that there are new, exciting projects being conceived in the arena of digital libraries, most notably the Digital Public Library of America, a new project of the Berkman Center for Internet & Society, launched in December 2010 with a grant from the Sloan Foundation. As of this writing, the project was still in the planning stage. More details can be found at *http://cyber.law.harvard.edu/research/dpla*.

A visit to the Googleplex

When we visited the Googleplex, our first interview was with James Crawford, an engineer with Google Books. I mentioned that the project had a number of applications for librarians and other researchers. I said that I had often used Google Books when tracing the authenticity of quotes. For instance, I had recently seen a mention of the line "Better to keep silent and let people think you a fool than to speak up and erase all doubt," which was attributed to Abraham Lincoln. I recognized that as something Mark Twain had said, so I set out to get the proof. In Google proper, there are thousands of attributions for each man, but in the public domain section of Google Books, we see that neither man said it. The saying first turns up in the 1907 children's book, *Mother Goose, her book*, by Maurice Switzer. Crawford by now had his laptop out checking out the story.

I asked him about the late summer ruling against Google, but he didn't know about any rulings beyond Judge Chin's. He thought that the matter was over when that ruling came down. One of the interesting plans in the Google Book settlement was the placement of special access machines in each academic or public library that would have full access to millions of copyrighted books. I asked if the ruling meant that this idea was dead forever, and Crawford acknowledged that it was. I asked if Google had a list of the post-1923 titles that had fallen out of copyright because of failures to renew. He said that they had not made such a list, but since the ruling they are paying more attention to that.

The Internet Archive

The Internet Archive was founded in 1996 by Spencer Kahle and Bruce Gilliat. Its purpose was to create a record of all iterations of web pages in the World Wide Web. They created the technology to do this and formed a separate for-profit company called Alexa Internet that crawls the web and supplies the data to the Archive. The company was bought in 1999 by Amazon.com, but it continues to supply the archive with page information. In 1999, the archived web pages became available to the public at the site using a link called the "Wayback Machine," named after a device found in the American TV animation series of the 1960s, *The Rocky & Bullwinkle Show*.

The Archive has started an active collection of book digitization. Its offerings are particularly interesting because of software Alexa Internet developed that simulates page turning in an actual book. By late 2011, the company was claiming that 1000 public domain volumes were being added every day, from the scanning center in its San Francisco offices and from scanning centers in 27 libraries in six countries. I asked Alexis Rossi, Web Collections Manager with Internet Archive some questions over email:

Ballard: Do you supply marc records to libraries?

Rossi: Generally we get MARC records from the libraries who we scan books for, and we have also received many large-scale dumps of MARC records for the OpenLibrary.org project (large dumps are in http://www.archive.org/details/ol_data). We're not really oriented toward being a source of MARC records (like OCLC is), but we have seen quite a bit of use regardless. In one case, a partner library uses their own MARC records from our website for various processing steps, rather than using their local catalog, because our version is more easily available and in different formats. We've done dumps of all books available for lending to give to partner libraries for incorporation in their OPACs. And I believe several non-library projects have used the records in bulk for their own projects. Any individual is also welcome to download the MARC records for books we've scanned, or the bulk dumps of MARC records.

Ballard: Our librarians were extremely impressed with the difference between your scanned titles and those of Google. What kind of technology are you using?

Rossi: We use a scanning system that we developed ourselves, called the Scribe. You can see it in this video: http://www.archive.org/details/ InternetArchive-Tour – the scribes are the black shrouded machines. Basically, there's a V-shaped platform that the book rests on which is covered by a V-shaped glass cover to keep the pages flat. There are two Canon cameras that point at the book page surfaces capturing both pages each time the operator clicks the shutter. A foot pedal raises and lowers the glass so that pages can be turned by hand. The raw images are uploaded to our servers along with cropping and deskewing information provided by human operators so that we can trim and orient the pages correctly for the best presentation. The process is non-destructive, and can be used on very old books (I think the oldest book we've done is from the 1300s). We do use commercial OCR software, but the rest of the process is home grown. I'm happy to provide more details on this if you'd like, including what happens before and after the book images are captured.

Ballard: Have you researched a list of titles that are post 1923 but still in the public domain due to nonrenewal?

Rossi: No, we don't feel that we are able to make copyright decisions.

Ballard: About your collection of a half million books. Where is it housed? Will there eventually be public access?

Rossi: The physical collection is housed in Richmond, California. Books are packed into book boxes and placed on pallets. The pallets live in shipping containers that have been modified to maintain heat and humidity levels conducive to preservation. As you can imagine, this storage model is not intended to provide easy access to the physical books on a one-by-one basis. That access happens through the online, scanned version of the book.

You can read more about the physical Archive and see pictures at *http://www.archive.org/about/about.php#why.* In September 2011, the day after our trip to the Googleplex, I visited Internet Archive's headquarters in the Richmond section of San Francisco. When I told my wife about the side trip, she admitted that she had not heard of Internet Archive, even though she is a public librarian. I told her, "Think of them as the Rebel Alliance." That got more laughs in San Francisco than it did in Mountain View. I was curious about how the Archive was funded, assuming that grants were a big part of it. Rossi told me that grants were a relatively small part of their income. They have to pay for services such as digitization and OCR for companies, and a program called Archive-It for intense archiving of an organization or company's web pages. Also she mentioned that Spencer Kahle still provides support for the operation.

After our talk, I got a tour of the facility, which looks like a giant ski lodge on the inside. Rossi led me to a separate building that houses their main scanning facility. The book scanners have overhead optics and the book sits on a device that gently turns the pages. It appeared that they could take a new shot about every ten seconds. Figure 10.7 shows a special machine that processes unusual formats such as pull-out maps.

I also got a good look at the quirky side of the Internet Archive when we visited the main hall where the company holds its local seminars and other events. The building used

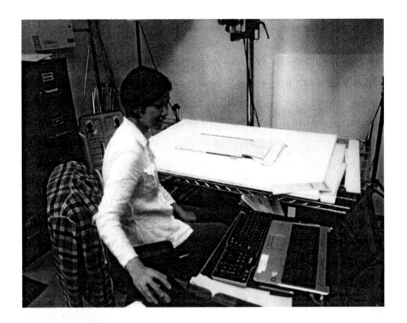

Figure 10.7 Scanning at the Internet Archive

Source: http://www.flickr.com/photos/terryballard/6717847325/in/photostream (accessed 17 January 2012) © Terry Ballard

to be a church and this was the main sanctuary, with the pews still intact. In the upper left-hand portion of the pews, I was shown "Terra Cotta Digitizers," modeled after the terracotta soldiers in China. Rossi explained that when a person had been employed at the Archive for three years, they get a statue made that will stay there in perpetuity.

A major project of the Archive is the Open Library. Funded in part by a grant from the State Library of California, the project is digitizing copyrighted or public domain books sent in by participating libraries, adding the paper copies to a storehouse facility, and sending the library a digital copy, which may then be checked out to its patrons like a physical book for two weeks. The idea has mushroomed in the past year, and in November of 2011 it was announced that the state libraries of all 50 US states had signed on to the effort.

The e-book revolution

By the late 1990s and early twenty-first century, publishers were experimenting with commercial electronic books that were available in addition to or instead of their paper offerings. This involved a period of experimentation with price structure and portable readers. It was a frustrating time for libraries, since no e-reader was superior enough to become the standard. It became fashionable around 2000 to hear "The e-book is dead." This changed dramatically in November of 2007 when Amazon launched its Kindle player. Users had a lot of complaints about this device, but Amazon couldn't make them fast enough. By 2012, the Kindle dominated the reader market in the way that the iPod dominated the music player market. With the color Kindle Fire priced at $200, Amazon could bundle its vast library of books, music and video to create a serious challenge to Apple. Although there are other good readers around, what Amazon created was a full paradigm shift.

Conclusion

We have seen that the world of text online has a specific beginning point – 4 July 1971, when Michael Hart sent the Declaration of Independence to a handful of technicians in research institutions. In the early twenty-first century, digitization of books was a common practice in universities, and they were making thousands of public domain books available to anyone with a networked computer, including titles that were extremely rare. Then in 2004 Google got involved and suddenly librarians were talking about millions of books instead of thousands. In San Francisco we have seen how the Internet Archive has created a healthy alternative to Google by working closely with libraries of all sizes. Finally we have seen how Amazon reversed a long trend of unsatisfactory e-book availability in libraries.

Webliography

42 Kindles – a discussion on the evolution of text:
https://docs.google.com/viewer?a=v&q=cache:94QsO92KWQYJ: journals.dartmouth.edu/cgi-bin/WebObjects/Journals.woa/2/ xmlpage/4/document/ 660+&hl=en&gl=us&pid=bl&srcid=ADG EESjjIOxpy 6dyQkrLqHsxIlTCYFhlHkQIDC5ZsAL9EtYQVP 5rN78NpGxHHS9bkRvWMou FrxNpK7R1KsHF&sig= AHIEtbTrMShErGFlNSz-td9HWYXSkkuIcw (accessed 2 March 2012).

About Google Books:
http://books.google.com/intl/en/googlebooks/history.html (accessed 2 March 2012).

All 50 state librarians vote to join the Internet Archives Open Library:
http://www.thedigitalshift.com/2011/11/ebooks/all-50-state- librarians-vote-to-form-alliance-with-internet-archives-open- library/ (accessed 2 March 2012).

Amazon Kindle article in Wikipedia:
http://en.wikipedia.org/wiki/Amazon_kindle (accessed 2 March 2012).

An GortaMor:
http://www.thegreathunger.org (accessed 2 March 2012).

Copyright and research in Google Book Search:
http://scholarship.law.wm.edu/cgi/viewcontent.cgi?article=102 6&context=libpubs&sei-redir=1&referer=http%3A%2F%2 Fscholar.google.com%2Fscholar%3Fhl%3Den%26q%3D% 2522history%2Bof%2Bgoogle%2Bbooks%2522%26btnG% 3DSearch%26as_sdt%3D0%252C33%26as_ylo%3D%26as_ vis%3D0#search=%22history%20google%20books%22 (accessed 2 March 2012).

Encyclopedia article about the Internet Archive:
http://ia700606.us.archive.org/22/items/internetarchive- encyclis/EncycLisInternetArchive.pdf (accessed 2 March 2012).

Google Book Search and the future of books in cyberspace:
*http://people.ischool.berkeley.edu/~pam/papers/GBSandBooks
InCyberspace.pdf* (accessed 2 March 2012).

Google Books Wikipedia article:
http://en.wikipedia.org/wiki/Google_books (accessed 2 March
2012).

Google NGram:
http://books.google.com/ngrams (accessed 2 March 2012).

History of Google Books:
http://books.google.com/intl/en/googlebooks/history.html
(accessed 2 March 2012).

In a flood tide of digital data, an ark full of books:
*http://www.nytimes.com/2012/03/04/technology/internet-
archives-repository-collects-thousands-of-books.html?_
r=1&pagewanted=all* (accessed 2 March 2012).

Online Books Page:
http://onlinebooks.library.upenn.edu/ (accessed 2 March 2012).

Project Gutenberg main page:
http://www.gutenberg.org/ (accessed 2 March 2012).

Timeline of the Open Access Movement:
*http://dash.harvard.edu/bitstream/handle/1/4724185/suber_
timeline.htm* (accessed 2 March 2012).

Wikipedia – Google Books:
http://en.wikipedia.org/wiki/Google_book_search (accessed 2
March 2012).

References

Ballard, T. and Donnald, E. (2007) "A Digitization and Multimedia
Project at Quinnipiac University, Hamden, Connecticut,
USA," *New Library World*, 108(9–10): 445–52.

Grimmelmann, J. (2009) The Google Book Search settlement:
Ends, means, and the future of books. Available at: *https://
www.acslaw.org/files/Grimmelmann%20Issue%20Brief.pdf*
(accessed 2 March 2012).

11

Discovery platforms

Abstract: Since web catalogs completely eliminated card catalogs in the 1990s there has been little substantive change in the way they work. All of them have the traditional card catalog searches, as well as keyword. There is an option to refine searches to bring in a more focused, manageable set, but extensive research has shown that this option is almost never taken. This chapter shows that as the twenty-first century saw the rise of Google, the expectations of library users changed, with more patrons being dissatisfied with the classic online catalog, which they saw as containing too much library jargon. It looks at the rise of a new type of catalog that overlaid the classic catalog and delivered a more intuitive look. It had tag clouds and facets to limit the results to certain types of material or locations. Since libraries were running both types of catalogs simultaneously, it was easy to find out if they were more likely to limit a search in a discovery catalog. Several libraries reported that users were 20 times more likely to refine a search in a discovery catalog.

Key words: AquaBrowser, discovery platforms, Encore, OPAC, Summon.

"Discovery is seeing what everybody else has seen, and thinking what nobody else has thought."

– Albert Szent-Gyorgyi, Hungarian physiologist and Nobel prize winner

Introduction

Since the text beginnings of online catalogs in libraries, users have been offered the choice of refining a search by location, year and format, but studies have shown that most patrons just look at what is before them and don't take the extra step. I wrote about this in 1994, studying search logs in the Adelphi University catalog. The study (Ballard, 1994) showed that searches made in the public catalog machines were limited about 1 per cent of the time by patrons. Searches done at the reference desk, presumably by librarians, were only limited 2 per cent of the time.

The rise of web catalogs in the late 1990s added more graphic capabilities and more choices for Online Public Access Catalog (OPAC) screens, but the functionality was little different – chiefly Author, Title and Subject searches with the addition of Keyword. The addition of the 856 field, which creates a link in the catalog record to take the user to a particular resource, allowed linking to resources beyond the library inside of a marc record. In 2000, however, the OPAC was more tied to card catalogs than web search engines. We started hearing complaints that the online catalog was out of step with the information needs of users who were raised on Google. Like their predecessors, the online catalog offered the ability to refine a search, but this was used rarely.

By 2005 there was a phrase sweeping the technology conferences: "Death of the OPAC." Perhaps it is not a coincidence that in the ensuing years we have seen the rise of "discovery platforms," overlays to classic catalogs that provide the kinds of services that users have come to expect using sites such as Amazon. These platforms include features such as tag clouds, facets to limit search results, community tagging, and reviewing. Harvard installed AquaBrowser from Serials Solutions and Encore from Innovative Interfaces for use with its library catalog, HOLLIS. Soon hundreds of libraries were adding these options, but there hasn't been much research into the matter of how they affect user behavior.

A new offering

When I was hired at the New York Law School I was told that the school had just signed up for Encore, the discovery platform from Innovative Interfaces (Figure 11.1). This was good news because I had already helped install the same service at my previous job (Ballard and Blaine, 2011).

Installation involved setting up a second server next to the main ILS server and linking the two. This was done in April, and there were several months of getting used to the new service before it was introduced to the librarian group in July, and released for public view the next month. I was interested in seeing usage log statistics on this, but Innovative Interfaces people told me the only option was to get set up with Google Analytics, which we did promptly.

Figure 11.1   Page results in an Encore search

Source: http://encore.nyls.edu/iii/encore/search?formids=target&lang=eng&suite=de f&reservedids=lang%2Csuite&submitmode=&submitname=&target=google&x=0&y=0 (accessed 17 January 2012) © New York Law School

There has been much discussion about letting patrons tag records in the library catalog – some librarians want to be more like Amazon; others see this as giving the keys to the inmates. I had never seen a real-world example of this until recently. The Ann Arbor District Library has not only opened tagging up to their patrons, but they make it look like something that really works. You can see the results at *http:// www.aadl.org/catalog*. This is useful for subjects where the controlled subject language from the Library of Congress is at odds with the way people think of subject terms – a classic case is the official term "Cookery," versus the term a normal person might use in a search: "Cookbook."

We also added a Google Analytics for our classic catalog so we could, to some extent, have a side-by-side comparison. Encore was mentioned in the first-year orientation sessions, so there was a good amount of log data to study. The results showed a substantial difference in usage. Over the past year there were 12 000 Encore sessions compared to 43 000 classic. The classic catalog had an 83 per cent bounce rate (users who got to the main screen but did not search anything) compared to a 33 per cent bounce rate in Encore. Classic users spent an average 90 seconds in their sessions compared with nearly 4 minutes for Encore users. Total searches were 51 000 for Encore and 57 000 for classic. Some of this can be explained by the fact that the Classic catalog front page features an Encore search bar (Figure 11.2). When a user makes that search it counts as a bounce on the classic catalog.

In our classic catalog we keep one year's worth of search log data. We found that users took advantage of the Refine this search button about one half of 1 per cent of the time. During that same period in Encore, we found that searches employed a facet or a tag cloud 8.5 per cent of the time, so at our library a user is about 15 times more likely to refine

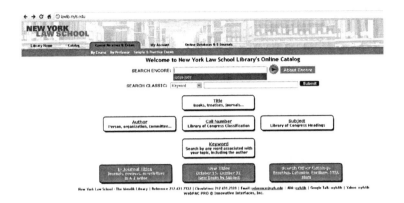

Figure 11.2   Example of a standard online catalog

Source: *http://lawlib.nyls.edu/* (accessed 17 January 2012)
© New York Law School

a search if they are in Encore. At first glance, we found this ratio startling, so we set out to get verification from similar libraries.

The most thorough verification was provided by the Wellcome Library, a foundation-based library in London. They also have an Innovative Interfaces ILS and Encore. In their classic catalog, out of more than 200 000 searches, only 600 were limited. Their Encore logs showed more than 10 per cent of searches used facets. Anne Prestamo from Oklahoma State University reported that more than 22 per cent of searches used some form of facet refinement in their AquaBrowser system. Beth Dempsey of Serials Solutions said that one of her clients, a large general university shared log data showing that nearly 50 per cent of searches used facets in a Summon search.

Tim Darlington of Massey University in New Zealand reported these numbers: "A quick look at Google Analytics for our Encore implementation shows 30,190 page views with 'facet' in the URL over the last month, varying between a low of 330 (on a weekend day) and 1650 (on a week day)." Darlington felt that this number was low but, as we have seen, very consistent with other Encore sites.

At the American Library Association 2011 meeting in New Orleans I was giving a brief presentation about this data. I mentioned that I had got information from one AquaBrowser user, and I had hoped to get information from Harvard, but I couldn't get anybody there to talk to me. From the front row a voice piped up – "I'm from Harvard and I'll talk to you." This was Corinna Baksik, who wrote the following extremely helpful information:

> According to the statistics package supplied by the vendor, the relative usage of the facets is shown here for May 2011. May is a heavy use period academically here, and the stats package says there were 200,000 sessions and 430,000 searches. We have done some separate tracking which reflects a lower usage for this period, but the facet hits below are from the same stats package as these session/search counts, so I think it's fair to use them for relative use of facets during searches. What this doesn't reflect is relative usage of Advanced Search vs. Basic search. Based on some anecdotal evidence (written user feedback), many folks like to limit the search in advance by using the Advanced Search, rather than using the facets post-search. AquaBrowser has a "search initiators" statistic, and according to that, 35% of searches during this period were initiated through the basic search box, and 46% were "other." It's my belief that the "other" reflects usage of our home-grown Advanced Search page, which constructs a search URL and sends it to AB [AquaBrowser].

Format	5155
Publication Date	4938
Author / Creator	3299
Language	2855
Online	2798
Location	2572

Social tagging

In 2010, we were preparing for the arrival of the New York Law School's most famous alum – Judith Sheindlin from the class of 1965. Her bio says that she has written six books, so I did a keyword search on "Judge Judy" and found two current titles displayed. However, when I did an author search for "Sheindlin," three of her titles came up. It turns out that there was a variation in the author information, and one of the titles had no reference to "Judge Judy." We had just purchased Encore, so I used this as a test case for "Social Tagging." I called up the book that had not displayed in keyword and clicked on Add a tag. I was reminded to log in. Once that happened, I got a data box to enter my own search for this title. I added "Judge Judy" and saved it. Then I searched in Encore and all of the titles came up. My understanding was that this would only happen when the machine was logged into my account. My understanding was wrong. The extra tag was present for everyone to use in a search.

I soon found out that this technique could have a more serious use. My director recently complained that a student searching in Encore got no hits for the Supreme Court case "Pennoyer v. Neff." While this case is mentioned in many of our books, there is no chapter title for it in the catalog, so the user came away with nothing. Without at least one hit, the student could not follow a link into WebBridge to search the case in other sources such as JSTOR or HeinOnline or even Google Books. To address this, I found a copy of the *Oxford Companion to the Supreme Court* and confirmed that this contained information about Pennoyer, so I logged in, called up that record and added a tag for Pennoyer. Now when anyone searches the catalog for Pennoyer, they get references and links to other sources through WebBridge. A committee of librarians is being formed to strategize the appropriate use of social tagging here.

At the East Meadow Public Library, reader services librarians were adding new features to their Facebook page. One of these was a report on the hottest best sellers coming out for the public every Tuesday. The first entry described three new titles, but left it to the patrons to go into the catalog and find them. Since the library has Encore, I suggested using the social tagging feature to mark the titles, save the URL and paste that into the Facebook entry as a link. They added the tag "newbook 020112" to each of the titles, and the link worked perfectly.

The Westerville Public Library in Ohio has long been known for its imaginative use of Innovative Interfaces products, so it was no surprise when I heard this from Tamara Murray: "Our staff are heavy users of Encore's tagging feature. We use it to create lists 'on the fly' for patrons for various assignments, to cover informal or lesser-known genres, to offer lists of staff picks and event tie-ins and more."

Lucy Clifford at City University London offered this example:

> We've tagged up our resource records in Encore to allow us to create canned subject based searches to "key" and "background" e-resources which we can then put into LibGuides (or anywhere else).

e.g. key aeronautics

background aeronautics

You can see some links here

http://libguides.city.ac.uk/content.php?pid=238813&si d=1970762

This seemed like a good way to avoid duplication of work. Our resource records usually contain good quality information so we don't need to duplicate this elsewhere and it's a quick and simple job to add or remove records from the lists.

Mina Edmondson of the York County Library System in Pennsylvania wrote:

At the York County Library System in Pennsylvania, we have tagged our local schools "Recommended Reading Lists." This helps students, parents and staff find items quicker. Adding tags to the list has also identified titles we need to purchase. We have also tagged some titles dealing with social issues. The first that comes to mind is "cutting." Self-mutilation is the term used in our subject headings. Telling a person who is brave enough to ask at the desk for books on cutting to look under self-mutilation is not responsive to their needs. The catalog is now able to direct them without unnecessary staff intervention. Of course, staff is available if needed. We are also beginning a project of tagging read alikes. Staff picks for wimpy kid fans...

Conclusion

Discovery platforms came with the promise of giving users a better idea of the choices they had in searching a catalog by pulling the choices out of secondary screens and placing them in the users' faces. The early research here shows that this is the effect that discovery platforms are having on users. There can be no doubt that the search limiting function in classic online catalogs is almost entirely ignored by users, and no amount of bibliographic instruction is likely to change this. Much more research needs to be done, but the results I've seen show that the discovery platforms are accomplishing what their makers hoped they would.

Webliography

Discovering linked data:
   http://www.libraryjournal.com/lj/ljinprintnetconnect/888240-335/ fiona_bradley_takes_a_tour.html.csp (accessed 2 March 2012).
Harvard University HOLLIS Catalog:
   http://hollis.harvard.edu/ (accessed 2 March 2012).
Massey University Library:
   http://www.massey.ac.nz/massey/research/library/library_home.cfm (accessed 2 March 2012).
New York Law School Classic and Discovery Catalog:
   http://lawlib.nyls.edu (accessed 2 March 2012).
Wellcome Library:
   http://catalogue.wellcome.ac.uk/ (accessed 2 March 2012).
Westerville Public Library social tagging examples:
   http://libftp.nyls.edu/westerville.html (accessed 2 March 2012).

References

Ballard, T. (1994) "Comparative search styles of staff and patrons," *Library Resources and Technical Services*, 38(3): 293–305.
Ballard, T. and Blaine, A. (2011) "User search-limiting behavior in online catalogs: Comparing classic catalog use to search behavior in next-generation catalogs," *New Library World*, 112 (5/6): 261–73.

12

Mobile applications for libraries

Abstract: This chapter shows how the world of mobile applications is exploding, while the use of these devices for libraries is still in its infancy. A look at the iTunes store, the BlackBerry store and the Android Market show that a handful of libraries are making a full service application available to search the catalog, check their library records, renew a book or access databases. A case study is presented that shows how a mobile application went from negotiations with the vendor until the day the final product was unveiled, including choice of graphics, set up of channels, and the loading of flat files to make for a speedier search of the catalog. The chapter discusses the relative merits of the major suppliers of mobile applications, including BiblioCommons (New York Public Library), Boopsie (New York Law School), and Library Anywhere from LibraryThing. It also shows how the case-study library developed a web-enabled catalog that could be accessed from a mobile phone without an application.

Key words: Android, Boopsie, InfoCommons, iPhones, Library Anywhere, mobile applications, smart phones.

"Simplify, simplify."

– Henry David Thoreau, American author and philosopher

The mobile universe

According to current statistics, there are 5.3 billion mobile phone users on the planet. That is 77 per cent of the world's population. Half a billion of these have already tried the mobile web. At the current rate of growth, 2016 will be the year that there will be more web traffic on mobile devices than on desktop and laptop computers combined.

Case study: the Mendik Library of New York Law School

Finding a provider

At the Mendik Library of New York Law School, we had, for years, discussed the prospect of adding a mobile application so users could search the catalog easily on public transportation or wherever they happened to be. The web services librarian, Grace Lee, pushed hard for this, and I'll admit that I just couldn't see the need. Our online catalog provider, Innovative Interfaces, had a product called AirPac, that would enable the catalog for mobile users, but it was prohibitively expensive.

At the Innovative Interfaces Users Group meeting of 2011 in San Francisco, the keynote speaker was Thomas Frey, director of the DaVinci Institute. In an outstanding presentation, he warned us about how the world was changing, about how standard cell phones are being rapidly replaced by smart phones, and how we are scant years from the time when the majority of traffic on the Internet will be through smart phones rather than standard computers. Further he explained that the number of mobile applications is growing at an exponential rate. There will be apps to monitor your blood pressure, turn on the lights before you get home and check the oil level in your car. Libraries had better keep an eye on this, because this is becoming the way that people are getting their information.

I came back to New York as a mobile believer. I started looking in the iTunes store and the Android Market to see what libraries had been doing. The answer was that I could only find a handful of university and public libraries in the stores. There was a mixed assortment of public libraries who had listed their homemade applications – obviously their library was lucky enough to have a programmer on board. From the university and large systems who were displaying applications, I began to search for the names of developers to see which one had the most activity.

At the next technology meeting of the library, I gave them a name that they had never heard of – "Boopsie." The repeated the name in sheer amazement. "Yes," I said, "the name that I keep seeing in the Apple and Android stores is Boopsie, Inc." This began a long process of communication with the company. We started looking at other catalogs that they had developed for libraries on Innovative Interfaces systems. In total, over the next few months our experience was similar to that described by Johnstone (2011). The applications looked attractive and useful, but we noticed that they all lacked one thing – course reserves. At the Mendik Library, this was a major part of the circulation process.

Creating the channels

In the meantime, I had met librarians from Ohio at the BookExpo conference in New York. Their library had just added Boopsie's application and they were extremely complimentary about it. Next month, I was at the American Library Association conference in New Orleans where

Boopsie had a booth. I talked to them about the reserves module. The short answer was that they had not developed one because no school had asked yet. It was important to us, so we started brainstorming ways to get them the data they would need. Days later, we got our answer. They had figured out a way to get the data directly off of the server. For the normal catalog collection, they needed a "flat file." This consisted of marc records exported from our catalog server and held for them on the library's open web server. This allows Boopsie to keep a mirror file of our collection. The practical result of this is that when a user starts typing "communic" the screen below starts filling up with every title that has the word communication. If the user selects that title to see more information, the program then goes to the catalog server and checks the status of the item.

We opened a special account in Google Docs so that all of us involved in the process could work on the files that went into developing the various mobile channels. In the case of some channels such as the one for library information, the web services librarian had to input all of the details. She also had to write all of the promotional material to describe the application for the mobile stores. In addition to Apple and Android, Boopsie also worked with the BlackBerry and Palm stores. Each of these had its own requirements for inclusion, but nobody had stranger rules than Apple.

Once the application was finished it was sent to the Apple store with a check for US$50 so that Apple could evaluate the application. The application for the Android store was processed within hours. While the Apple stores were considering our case, the application had gone live, and Boopsie had provided us with a page to point to. When users aimed their smart phones at this page it discerned what type of device they were using and sent them to the appropriate store (Figure 12.1).

Figure 12.1 Preview of the mobile application

Source: http://www.nyls.edu/library/mendik_mobile_app/
(accessed 11 March 2012) © New York Law School

Launching the product

In September, 2011, we began the process of advertising the service on campus. From the various sources we had for measuring usage, it was an immediate hit. We discovered at this time that while other law school libraries had developed mobile-enabled catalogs and other services, we were the first law school library in the world to publish a full service application that was found in all of the major stores. This culminated in a group shot at the reference desk with librarians holding up their smart phones (Figure 12.2).

During the summer that we were developing the mobile application, we were also investigating a parallel project – a mobile-enabled online catalog. This means that we wanted to give users the ability to call up the catalog on their mobile devices, and have their service automatically redirected to a mobile catalog. To begin the process, I found a few people with Innovative Interfaces catalogs who had written about doing this and giving instructions on how to make it happen.

Figure 12.2 New York Law School librarians holding their cell phones to launch the new service
© Terry Ballard

The most promising of these came from Pennsylvania, and they gave instructions mainly for the Information Technology people on our campus who ran our network. I had to re-edit one file on the library server, and they had to make four or five adjustments. Then the day came, and it didn't work at all.

I kept asking around. The people who had written the directions were no longer at that school, and had left no forwarding address. I asked Bob Duncan, an automation librarian known for his extreme knowledge of systems and his helpfulness. He gave me a few clues, but we were getting no results still. Once the Boopsie catalog went live, I tried to borrow code from the demonstration screen above to create a simple catalog. The results were not pretty. I called Gary Fletcher from Boopsie and told him my problem. He let me know that they had already created a web-enabled catalog. We could see it by directing our devices to *m.lawlib.nyls.edu*, and would get perfectly proportioned catalog data.

This should have been the end of the problem, but the library's associate director insisted on a system that would cause the incoming request to the regular catalog to be recognized as mobile and then redirected to the mobile version. I did more asking around and found that it was mainly a matter of adding a few lines of code to the main menu of the catalog. The school's assistant webmaster finally found what we needed, and now the page is fully functional.

After some investigation, it turned out that this kind of functionality is fairly rare. Going to the major broadcast television stations on a mobile device shows you that only CBS automatically directs to a mobile-enabled screen. However, the others display correctly if you type "m." and then the rest of their URL.

Library Anywhere

Library Anywhere is a product of LibraryThing. I spoke with the company's president, TimSpalding, at the American Library Association. He mentioned that they were providing mobile applications for a number of libraries. Later on, when I made the searches of "public library" or "university library" in the Apple store, I saw that there were a number of listings for Boopsie or BiblioCommons, a few homemade applications, but nothing for Library Anywhere. Later, I tried searching just "library anywhere" and found that the libraries are listed inside the application. Indeed, there are quite a few. I found a number of sites in upstate New York, and when looking at the individual libraries, I did not see a catalog search specifically. I emailed Spalding to ask about this and was informed that all of the Library Anywhere applications included a catalog interface – the search bar at the top of the screen did that, even though there was not a "channel" listed for online catalog.

Recently I found out that a library that I am connected with in the Midwest had an application from Library

Anywhere. In this case, there was a Catalog channel as the first option. I asked a friend there about their experience with this application, and was told that their technical support was outstanding, and the librarians loved the price. I found literature showing that the service started at just over US$100, and reached a maximum of about a US$1000. This makes it a bargain, indeed. I think Library Anywhere has a promising future – particularly with budget-minded public libraries.

BiblioCommons

BiblioCommons is a Toronto-based company that has made impressive strides in the market for discovery platforms, and now it is making a presence in the mobile library market. In 2011, BiblioCommons developed a mobile application for the New York Public Library. The company is providing the mobile applications for a number of Canadian libraries – most notably Vancouver, Windsor and Hamilton.

The mobile market

I had an email conversation with Greg Carpenter, the president of Boopsie, Inc. about the state of the mobile library market near the end of 2011. I volunteered an opinion that 90 per cent of libraries in the United States had not committed to a mobile supplier yet, and that within three years the majority of libraries would have a working application of some sort. Here is what he had to say:

> You are probably correct regarding the number of public libraries that do not have a mobile presence. We have about 250 libraries for which we have created

mobile apps – which is pretty small in comparison to the total number out there. However, the larger libraries are eager to get moving, so we have 10 of the top 12 libraries on the Hennen list as customers. Smaller libraries find it difficult to create their own mobile presence due to a lack of tools available to them. Over time, the ILS vendors will be adding mobile-friendly features, but they are slow to move at this point – and they don't provide a full set of features for the library, only catalog access. We've found that over 50% of the use of our library mobile apps is for non-catalog information – like hours, locations, events, etc. We make it as simple as possible for smaller libraries to utilize the Boopsie platform at a reasonable annual cost compared to hiring anyone internally to create their mobile presence.

Given the rapid increase in e-book downloads, libraries are going to have to think "mobile" very quickly. In addition, without going "mobile," they are going to lose their younger patrons very quickly. We are seeing a steady increase in e-book downoads from mobile devices for our customers that have deployed our OverDrive integration into their mobile app. The integration simplifies access to the e-books from OverDrive. There are a couple of issues to consider as a public library tries to go mobile:

1. Do you create your mobile presence in-house, or use a 3rd party vendor like Boopsie.
2. Budget.

Given the diversity of mobile devices out there (which is creating a very fragmented market), the build vs. buy decision is a tricky one. Regardless of what path the library chooses, there is an impact on the budget. Most library budget cycles are annual, so a library may not be able to move forward for the next year, which will delay mobile roll-outs overall. So, your 3 year estimate is probably about right.

The younger audience is an "app based" culture, so they are moving away from browser based access to library resources. We track use of our services and have found that more younger people are using Android devices over any other device, with iPhone coming in just behind Android. However, the public sector "at large" is using more iPhone devices by a wider margin over Android vs. the younger segment. In the younger segment, there is an overall decrease in browser usage, but in the "older" segment, there is a slight increase in mobile browser use. Overall, this is indicating to us that the younger population is entrenched in using downloadable apps vs. the browser. So, libraries are going to have to look at that fact to provide services in a way that their up and coming patrons desire.

As an interesting aside, we are hearing libraries mention their budgets shifting from physical inventory to their e-books collections – Seattle Public Library has a very large selection of epubs available, for example.

As for WorldCat Mobile – they were one of our first customers. We started talking to Pepperdine University about 3–4 years ago and they recommended we speak with OCLC to look into partnering broadly across all libraries. We contacted OCLC and spoke with Cindy Cunningham in business development and we formed our partnership with them. Cindy knew mobile was going to grow quickly and OCLC did not have a mobile strategy at that time. So, we created WorldCat Mobile as the first foray into mobile. We would have liked to create a slightly different application, but OCLC was pretty slow to move on their end, so we ended up with a "reasonable" app, but we could have made it much better. OCLC has since decided to move that technology "in house" and they have created a mobile web site for WorldCat. However, we have many customers that prefer our app vs. the OCLC mobile site. The upside of the application was that OCLC realized that mobile was going to come around much quicker than they first thought – which has proven to be very true.

Conclusion

We see two curves at work here. One shows exponential growth for the world of smart phones. Then you have a much gentler curve of libraries beginning to get involved. When the day arrives that more Internet is accessed through mobile than standard computers, we wouldn't want to be working at a library that did not provide this service.

Webliography

The case for home-grown, sustainable next generation library services: *http://www.hiddenpeanuts.com/postfiles/The%20case%20for% 20home-grown,%20sustainable%20nex%20%20Chad%20H aefele.pdf* (accessed 2 March 2012).
Gallery of mobile apps and sites: *http://www.nlm.nih.gov/mobile/* (accessed 2 March 2012).
Latest mobile statistics: *http://mobithinking.com/mobile-marketing-tools/latest-mobile-stats* (accessed 2 March 2012).

Library in your pocket: Strategies and techniques for developing successful mobile services:
http://www.educause.edu/Resources/LibraryinYourPocketStrategies a/195003 (accessed 2 March 2012).

Library mobile applications – What counts as success:
http://www.oclc.org/research/publications/library/2011/washburn-io.pdf (accessed 2 March 2012).

M-Libraries: Library success – a best practices wiki:
http://www.libsuccess.org/index.php?title=M-Libraries (accessed 2 March 2012).

Spectrum: Mobile learning, libraries and technology:
http://mobile-libraries.blogspot.com/ (accessed 2 March 2012).

There's an app for that! Libraries and mobile technology – an introduction to public policy considerations:
http://www.ala.org/offices/sites/ala.org.offices/files/content/ oitp/publications/policybriefs/mobiledevices.pdf (accessed 2 March 2012).

References

Johnstone, B. (2011) "Boopsie and librarians: Connecting mobile learners and the library," *Library Hi Tech News*, 28(4): 18– 21.

13

Where is this all going?

Abstract: This chapter discusses the ways that libraries can cope with the information revolution. It shows how the pace of information change is growing exponentially and the qualities that new librarians will need to possess to give high-quality library service. It shows some of the innovative ways in which libraries have used web technologies to better serve the information needs of their patrons. In particular it highlights the work of librarians at the Mentor Public Library in Ohio, which addressed a staff cut by adding an avatar in the form of a talking cat that occupies the library's main page and answers basic questions about the library as well as providing chatty asides. The conclusion of this chapter and this book is that there is an information tsunami occurring. It is not going to go away, so libraries need to either use it to their advantage or risk being swept away.

Key words: CD ROM, DVD, information strategies, qualities of next generation librarians.

"Keep an eye to the future, an ear to the past, and after thinking it over notice nothing much lasts."

– Robert Hunter, American singer-songwriter, the Grateful Dead

Introduction – the information shift

Years ago, while working in a public library, I had the job of adding item records to old books in the Arizona History room of the Phoenix Public Library. One book I ran across in passing was the 1895 college catalog for what is now the University of Arizona in Tucson. I happened to look at the requirements for entrance and couldn't believe what I was seeing. A prospective college student in 1895 was expected to solve quadratic equations, read classics in the original Latin and Greek, and translate works in French. Shortly afterwards, I moved to New York and didn't have access to these catalogs, so I couldn't answer the next question on my mind: "What did they learn after that when they went to college?"

Recently, I found a similar listing thanks to Google's exploding book digitization project (Brown University, 1895[1849]). Here are more qualifications for Brown:

> "Translation at sight of ordinary pages from Caesar."
>
> "Ovid, 2500 lines."
>
> "Translation into Latin of a continuous passage of English narrative, prepared from some portion of the prescribed prose."

In mathematics, the students only needed to know factors, common divisors and multiples, fractions, ratios and proportions, negative quantities and the interpretation of negative results, the doctrine of exponents, radicals and equations involving radicals, the binomial theory. What happened? Starting in 1895, the information needs of society shifted just a tiny bit every day – so slowly that nobody noticed until you looked at things over time. It's like watching the moon go across the sky – you can't notice it move, but if you do something for 10 minutes and look back up you'll see that it moved a lot. It is the information shift at work. Sometimes things speed up due to major informational events such as the invention of the World Wide Web or the smart phone revolution. We call these "Information Earthquakes."

The end of spin

Even before Netflix had great success with streaming video, it appeared to me that the DVD is becoming obsolete, along with the CD-ROM, cassette tapes, VHS and the phonograph record. My wife checked me out something from her library – a device called a "Playaway." It is an audio book on an iPod-like device that is devoted to that single title. No moving parts. Just hit the play button every morning and it picks up where it left off on the 5:19 train the night before. For the record, my initial book was John Grogan's *Marley and Me*.

Nine years ago when Arnold Bernhard library first opened at Quinnipiac University, the reference desk was famous for a box of floppy disks which were freely distributed to students who forgot theirs. It was not a unique experience to hear from a student holding up a floppy disk, saying "My whole semester's project is on this, and now I'm getting an error message." By the time I left, floppies had disappeared in favor of flash drives carried on keychains or worn around the neck. They may fail someday too, but I haven't heard about it. The most welcome improvement in computers would be getting rid of hard disks. When a computer boots up today, it does the same thing that it did in the 1980s – checks the hard drive, loads a number of processes, and finally lets you do something. The main difference is that the number of processes has increased exponentially. I've never heard anything that explained to me why a computer can't start up like an iPod: power it up and it's ready to work. Google actually tried this with a laptop called the Chromebook, but it didn't seem to have much impact.

Marshall Keys

Marshall Keys, library visionary, spoke at a conference I attended a few years ago in Massachusetts, putting digitization work in a Library 2.0 perspective. He started with the understatement that "Recall in Google is greater than precision." He told of the perceptions of the library that evolved in his days of being a librarian, starting with the concept that the library is a warehouse for books to the current concept that the library is a server farm where we keep the data. Automation progresses from "We do things differently" to "We do different things." Libraries must adopt a strategy of constant change – all life is beta. Libraries need to meet the emerging needs of their users.

Keys noted that if we don't adapt, we will face competition on all sides from commercial interests who do understand the current generation. A good example is Book Swim (*http://www.bookswim.com/*), which rents out books in the way that Netflix rents out movies. After a monthly subscription fee customers can keep any book as long as they want, but there is a preset limit as to the number of books out at any given time. Keys mentioned the Westerville Public Library in Ohio as an example of Library 2.0 that does not result in a loss of control or image. The library, already well known to me as a super user of Innovative Interfaces technology, has a motto "Busier than a freakin' Wal-Mart." Not your grandmother's public library. One of the things they did that caught my eye was checking out DVDs to teens along with DVD-viewing goggles and headsets.

What can go wrong?

Kay Cahill of the Vancouver Public Library in Canada wrote me about some of the things that come up when a library runs an extremely active social media program:

> We have had a number of issues, primarily on Facebook, around individuals using our wall to promote or sell

specific products or services. It never developed into a full-scale spam problem, but we do now remove such posts as a matter of course because there were enough of them that they were beginning to affect the user experience. We have tightened up the guidelines around this as part of our social media policy, and formalized them by posting them on our website as well as on Facebook. *http://www.vpl.ca/index.php/about/details/social_media_terms_of_use*

An interesting side issue that we've experienced a couple of times is the spread of erroneous information via social media. One example of this was in the aftermath of the Stanley Cup riot, when an incorrect rumor that the Children's Library had been destroyed by rioters was reported on Twitter and subsequently spread like wildfire. (The Children's Library actually suffered a broken window, necessitating the replacement of a pane of glass and some minor cleanup.) The original poster, when challenged, claimed that her source was a library employee. In spite of the fact that we used the official VPL account to advise her that this wasn't accurate, and explained that we were currently in the building and fully aware of the extent of damage, she continued to insist that her information was correct. The issue was put to bed when one of our staff took a picture of the open Children's Library with its single boarded up window to share with our users. We've since had a couple of similar instances, and learned that the best way of dealing with them is to move very swiftly before the story has a chance to spread far. The speedy response required to successfully manage the social media rumor mill is sometimes at odds with the more formal and hence slower response of an official press release from our Marketing & Communications department, so when sensitive issues are at stake we work with them closely on wording and appropriate information to share.

Even though we expect Google to be around for quite some time, the company is famous for trying out products and parting with the less popular ones. In my visit to Mountain View I asked a Google product manager about the absence of a government information search and was told that products that aren't popular enough don't last.

The case of MySpace.com

At its height in 2008, MySpace was the premiere social media site in the world, with a visit count higher than that of Google. Libraries everywhere opened up accounts and used this new way of communicating. Then Facebook changed from being a school-oriented site to one that gave open access to all. MySpace numbers began to fall and then virtually collapse. Looking at library sites in MySpace is visiting an electronic ghost town. Libraries did not close their accounts – rather, they just stopped maintaining them. Last entries are older for college libraries because they had moved their efforts to Facebook before the general population was allowed in.

The look of a digital library

Years ago, I developed a program to promote digital reference books by creating screens that simulated the look of walking into a library and choosing a book. Some people thought this was interesting, but the idea never really caught on (Figures 13.1 and 13.2).

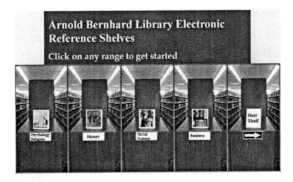

Figure 13.1 A virtual reference department

Source: *http://learn.quinnipiac.edu/verso/versomain.html*
(accessed 17 January 2012) © Quinnipiac University

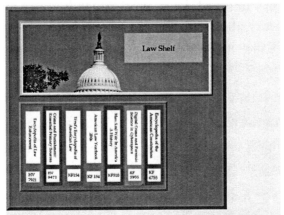

Figure 13.2 Example of one of the shelves

Source: *http://learn.quinnipiac.edu/verso/versolaw.html*
(accessed 17 January 2012) © Quinnipiac University

Google has taken this concept to a new level, inventing a digital book rack in the form of an eternal helix that can hold tens of thousands of titles (Figure 13.3).

Figure 13.3   How Google's virtual bookshelf may soon look

Source: http://popsop.com/50392 (accessed 2 March 2012) © Google, Inc.

The next generation of librarians

In March 2012, a Google search for "Digital Resources Librarian" returned more than 100 000 hits. One of the finer library observers, Stephen Abram (2007) describes the qualities that we might look for in the next generation of librarians. Here are some of them:

- Understands the power of the Web 2.0 opportunities.
- Learns the major tools of Web 2.0 and library 2.0.
- Combines e-resources and print formats seamlessly.
- Is container and format agnostic.
- Is device independent and uses and delivers to everything from laptops to PDAs (personal digital assistants) to iPods.
- Develops targeted federated search and adopts the OpenURL standard.
- Embraces non-textual information and the power of pictures, moving images, sight and sound.
- Sees the potential in using content sources such as the Open Content Alliance, Google Book Search and Open WorldCat.

- Uses the latest tools of communication (such as Skype) to connect content, expertise, information coaching and people.
- Uses and develops advanced social networks to enterprise advantage.
- Connects with everyone using their communication mode of choice – telephone, Skype, IM (instant messaging), SMS (short message service), texting, email, virtual reference, and so on.
- Encourages user-driven metadata and user-developed content and commentary.
- Mines usage data for insights into user behaviors.

There is a public library in Ohio whose work seems emblematic of this new kind of librarianship. When you go to the web page of the Mentor Public Library, you will see infoTabby "Emma," an animated talking library cat (Figure 13.4). I visited Emma

Figure 13.4   Emma the infoTabby

Source: http://www.infotabby.org/p/talk-with-infotabby.html
(accessed 12 March 2012) © David Newyear

recently. She sat staring ahead and blinking her eyes while waiting for me to ask her something. I typed "Dogs." She told me how to go to the catalog and make a keyword search, and then volunteered that some of her best friends were dogs. In a presentation at the 2011 Innovative Users Group meeting in San Francisco, Emma's creator, David Newyear, said that she was born out of the need to do more with less as the public library budgets in Ohio were shrinking. Emma performs basic triage for users in a way that they love.

Conclusion

We are in the midst of an information tsunami. Libraries can either embrace the best of the new tools, or resist and get swept away. From what I have seen, most libraries are open to the idea of a great use of social media, but most haven't done as much as they could, possibly because they don't know how to make things work. It is my hope that this book has opened a few doors for those libraries. After more than 50 years of being a library observer, I am very optimistic about the future of libraries. In communities, schools and colleges, the media have changed, but the library is still at the center of the search for information.

Webliography

Future of libraries and librarians:
  http://www.collegeonline.org/library/librarians-online/future-librarians.html (accessed 2 March 2012).
Future of libraries in the e-book age:
  http://www.npr.org/2011/04/04/135117829/the-future-of-libraries-in-the-e-book-age (accessed 2 March 2012).

Librarian 2.0 – Interviews of the future of librarians: *http://www.collegeonline.org/library/librarians-online/index. html* (accessed 2 March 2012).

Mentor Public Library: *http://www.mentorpl.org/catbot.html* (accessed 2 March 2012).

Off Campus Library Services keynote address: *http://distlib.blogs.com/distlib/2006/04/off_campus_libr.html* (accessed 2 March 2012).

The future of libraries; with or without books: *http://articles.cnn.com/2009-09-04/tech/future.library. technology_1_metropolitan-library-librarians-books?_s=PM: TECH* (accessed 2 March 2012).

Visualizing the library of the future: *http://www.davinciinstitute.com/papers/the-future-of-libraries-interview-with-thomas-frey/* (accessed ?).

Web 2.0, library 2.0 and librarian 2.0: preparing for the 2.0 world: *http://www.online-information.co.uk/online09/files/ freedownloads.new_link1.1080622103251.pdf* (accessed 2 March 2012).

References

Abram, S. (2007) "Web 2.0, library 2.0 and librarian 2.0: Preparing for the 2.0 world," in *Online Information 2007* (Day 1, Track 3). Available at: *http://www.online-information.co.uk/online09/ files/freedownloads.new_link1.1080622103251.pdf* (accessed 11 March 2012).

Brown University (1895[1849]) Requirements for admission. Available at: *http://books.google.com/books?id=h2XEXwEvc hwC&pg=PA16&dq=%22brown+university%22+catalog++ +greek+quadratic+virgil+translate&hl=en&sa=X&ei=NRBU T7OiCKX40gH43bHNDQ&ved=0CEIQ6AEwAA#v=onep age&q&f=false* (accessed 2 March 2012).

Bibliography

Agee, J. (2007) "Globalization, Digitization, Access, and Preservation of Cultural Heritage," *New Library World*, 108(5/6): 289–91.

Ballard, T. (2009) "Inheriting the earth: Using KML files to add placemarks relating to the library's original content to Google Earth and Google Maps," *New Library World*, 110(7/8): 357–65.

Bechera, M. and Schmidt, K. (2011) "Taking discovery Systems for a Test Drive," *Journal of Web Librarianship*, 5(3): 199–219.

Becker, C. (2009) "Student Values and Research: Are Millennials Really Changing the Future of Reference and Research?" *Journal of Library Administration*, 49(4): 341–64.

Hane, P. (2011) "Mobile Solutions for Libraries," *Information Today*, 28(6): 8.

Hill, V. and Lee, H. (2009) "Libraries and immersive learning environments unite in Second Life," *Library Hi Tech*, 27(3): 338–56.

Polanka, S. (2011) *No shelf required: e-books in libraries*. Chicago, American Library Association.

Index

CPSIA information can be obtained at www.ICGtesting.com
Printed in the USA
LVOW10s0154210214

374623LV00004B/38/P

201052